"Clever . . . witty."
—*Miami Herald*

"Offers not-always-obvious suggestions for, and pithy thumbnails of, great chick flicks . . ."
—*Morning Star-Telegram* (Fort Worth, Texas)

"Fun."
—*Body & Soul*

"A fun read and a great female-friendly guide for movie buffs."
—*Weight Watchers* magazine

"Movies as medication."
—*Toronto Sun*

"Peske and West know their movies."
—*Daily Breeze*

"Lighthearted . . . breezy, chatty style."
—*Publishers Weekly*

"A specialized version of Leonard Maltin, suggesting movies as
a way to combat the blues."
—*The Hackensack Record*

"Irreverent."
—*Style Weekly*

"It's nicely done and, like a fresh cup of popcorn, really hard to put down."
—*The Hartford Courant*

Also by Nancy Peske and Beverly West

Cinematherapy for Lovers: The Girl's Guide to Finding True Love One Movie at a Time

Advanced Cinematherapy: The Girl's Guide to Finding Happiness One Movie at a Time

Bibliotherapy: The Girl's Guide to Books for Every Phase of Our Lives

Cinematherapy: The Girl's Guide to Movies for Every Mood

Frankly, Scarlett, I *Do* Give a Damn!: Classic Romances Retold

And under the pseudonym Lee Ward Shore

How to Satisfy a Woman Every Time on Five Dollars a Day

Meditations for Men Who Do Next to Nothing (and Would Like to Do Even Less)

And by Beverly West

Culinarytherapy: The Girl's Guide to Food for Every Mood

Cinematherapy for the Soul

The Girl's Guide to Finding
Inspiration One Movie at a Time

Nancy Peske and Beverly West

DELTA TRADE PAPERBACKS

CINEMATHERAPY FOR THE SOUL
A Delta Book/February 2004

Published by Bantam Dell
A Division of Random House, Inc.
New York, New York

Book design by Virginia Norey

Library of Congress Cataloging-in-Publication Data

Peske, Nancy K., 1962–
    Cinematherapy for the soul : the girl's guide to finding inspiration one movie at a time / Nancy Peske and Beverly West.
        p.   cm.
    Includes index.
    ISBN 0-385-33704-3
    1. Motion pictures for women—Catalogs. 2. Video recordings—Catalogs. I. West, Beverly, 1961– II. Title

PN1995.9.W6 P477 2004
791.43/75/083 22   2003055827

Manufactured in the United States of America
Published simultaneously in Canada

RRH   10 9 8 7 6 5 4 3 2 1

To the moviemakers who picture peace and teach us that
changing the world starts with changing your perspective

Acknowledgments

A heartfelt thanks to our agent, Neeti Madan, our personal ambassador for peace; our editor, Danielle Perez, for her faith and her divine endurance; and our publicists, Theresa Zoro and Shawn Gallagher, for their unflagging optimism and enthusiasm.

Beverly would like to thank:

Ellen Rees, Joe Kolker, Susan Baumel Cornicello, and Laurie Green. A very special thanks to my cuz Nancy Peske, and to Jason Bergund, the best couchmate a girl ever had.

Nancy would like to thank:

Carol Peske, Sally Powell, Lindsey Biel, and all my friends and family. And as always, I'd like to thank George and Dante for letting me hog the big TV.

Contents

Introduction   *xiii*

Chapter 1   This Little Light of Mine: Shining Out Movies   *1*

Chapter 2   Like a Phoenix from the Ashes: Come On Up,
We're Rising Movies   *16*

Chapter 3   Side by Side: Finding Your Soul Mate Movies   *35*

Chapter 4   The Buck Stops Here: Accepting Personal
Responsibility Movies   *54*

Chapter 5   "Help! Jane! Stop This Crazy Thing!":
Antianxiety Movies   *72*

Chapter 6   The Call of the Wild: Getting Back to Nature Movies   *98*

Chapter 7   You Can Change the World: Power of One Movies   *120*

Chapter 8   All That Glitters Isn't Gold: Keeping It Real Movies   145

Chapter 9   My Karma Ran Over My Dogma: Letting Go of
             Your Status Quo Movies   160

Chapter 10   All Together Now: Love Is All Around You Movies   181

Index   207

Introduction

As all modern truth seekers and soul searchers understand, movies are more than entertainment: They're important tools that can inspire us to grow, motivate us to search for greater meaning in our daily lives, and enhance our spiritual well-being—all through the creative use of the remote control.

Has your inner glow been experiencing a brownout? Crank up the wattage with one of our Shining Out Movies and let your light out from under that bushel. Are you beginning to wonder if yours is the only soul in the universe that wasn't created as part of a matched pair? Curl up with one of our Finding Your Soul Mate Movies and learn to mix and match. Has your grudge gotten too heavy to bear? Take a load off with an Accepting Personal Responsibility Movie and learn to demand your fair share.

In our three previous *Cinematherapy* books, we've explored the ways that movies can put us in touch with our emotions, give us perspective on the issues that confront us in our daily lives, help us resolve conflicts, replenish our relationships, and grow from our life experiences without ever getting up off the couch except maybe to refill the popcorn bowl every once in a while. In **Cinematherapy for the Soul**, we explore how movies can inspire, guide, and comfort us as we make our way along the path toward inner peace.

So whether you're paralyzed with anxiety over what the future will bring, or hungry to make a difference but not sure what you can do to change your corner of the world, the movies in this guide will offer you examples of heroes and heroines who face their fears, rise from the ashes, discover their talents, and find love, light, laughter, and serenity.

Complete with inspirational quotes, recipes to feed your spiritual hunger, self-pampering rituals to rekindle your joie de vivre, and cautions against "junk food for the soul" movies that lead us away from the light, **Cinematherapy for the Soul** is guaranteed to help you discover the movies that will inspire, refresh, uplift, and reinvigorate your tired spirit and put you in touch with your authentic self, one movie at a time.

Cinematherapy for the Soul

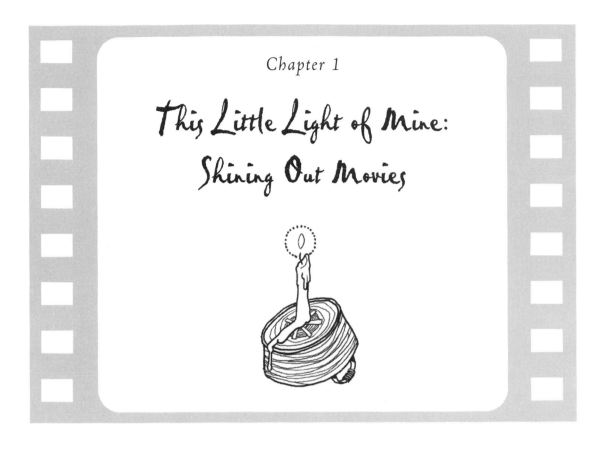

Chapter 1

This Little Light of Mine: Shining Out Movies

Has the shining city on your hill been experiencing a brownout? Have the lights in your personal display window been suddenly extinguished, leaving your best merchandise in the dark? We all have those days when we feel marked down for clearance. But don't worry, all it takes to inflate your value is a little self-appreciation and some regular downtime well spent with some of these Shining Out Movies, featuring heroes and heroines who take their moment front and center in the display case of life and demand what they're worth. They reassure us all that when we replace fear with love and let our light shine, we can name our price.

▪ *Grace of My Heart* (1996)
Stars: Illeana Douglas, John Turturro, Matt Dillon
Director and Writer: Allison Anders

Sometimes shining out is simply a matter of stepping out from behind somebody else's shadow. Illeana Douglas stars as Edna Buxton, a young singer and songwriter in the heyday of Tin Pan Alley, when men were men and girl groups were unemployed. Edna is forced to sell her songs rather than sing them herself and must wait for the day when the world will turn and she can record her own songs. Unfortunately, her world starts revolving around difficult men instead, and Edna winds up in a series of disastrous emotional and creative collaborations that serve only to dim her personal wattage until at last she is able to stand on her own two feet, sing her own songs, and cast her own long shadow.

Grace of My Heart is one of those rare movies that manages to fit the entirety of the female experience into two hours and four minutes, minus titles and credits, and for that reason it's one of our top ten, best all-around *Cinematherapy* movies. It's like an anthem to the resilience of the female spirit. So when your joie de vivre is flagging, watch *Grace of My Heart* and shine from the inside out.

▪ *The Gift* (2000)
Stars: Cate Blanchett, Giovanni Ribisi, Keanu Reeves, Katie Holmes,
  Michael Jeter, Greg Kinnear, Hilary Swank
Director: Sam Raimi
Writers: Billy Bob Thornton, Tom Epperson

It's hard for Annie Wilson (Cate Blanchett), single mom of three, to make ends meet. After all, she's just a small-town psychic who works with a deck of tarot cards in her kitchen—apparently she's unaware of the income-generating potential of a 900-number network and an ad in the back of *The National Enquirer*. Yet Annie does her best to keep her finances in the black and give her neighbors some glimpse into what the future holds for them. But when Annie starts experiencing terrifying dreams and visions of a dead woman shortly after the town floozy (Katie Holmes) disappears, her life gets very complicated. Suddenly everyone wants Annie to bend her talents to their will and come up with a nice, linear time scenario for an unsolved crime. Frankly, they want to hear about Colonel Mustard in the billiard room with the rope, not some poetic description of white lilies near a split-rail fence and a lifeless girl in a tree. Try though she might, Annie can't deliver, and it's starting to seem like all her efforts to be helpful to her neighbors are pathetically inadequate. Meanwhile, she's blinded to the grave danger she could be in.

When you're having a hard time appreciating your unique gifts, this movie will remind you that all talents, when embraced and nurtured, will produce benefits—but you may not be able to predict the outcomes with complete accuracy. So go on: Place that lantern on top of a bushel and let its light shine out for everyone.

And Then There Was Light

The only thing that moves here is the light, but it changes everything.
★ Nicole Kidman as Grace in *The Others*

Yet all the suns that light the corridors of the universe shine dim before the blazing of a single thought.
★ Arthur Kennedy as Dr. Duval in *Fantastic Voyage*

Remember, the shadows are just as important as the light.
★ Charlotte Gainsbourg as Jane in *Jane Eyre*

Bev's Culinarytherapy: Bring Out Your Inner Glow Goop

When you're feeling the need to emotionally exfoliate, try this food facial, which is guaranteed to help you throw off that dead skin and let your fresh face shine through. And you can even lick the bowl afterward!

Here's what you'll need:

1 ripe avocado	2 tablespoons sour cream
Juice of ½ lemon	½ teaspoon salt

Here's how you do it:

Peel and pit the avocado, and mash it with a fork. Stir in the lemon juice, sour cream, and salt. Apply to your entire face, and let it sit for about 20 minutes, then gently wipe off the goop with a damp cloth and bask in your own glow. Eat the remaining goop with chips and a little salsa.

▪ *Little Voice* (1998)
Stars: *Jane Horrocks, Brenda Blethyn, Michael Caine, Ewan McGregor*
Director: *Mark Herman*
Writer: *Mark Herman, based on the play by Jim Cartwright*

If the volume control on your little corner of the world has been cranked to eleven lately, and you're finding it hard to hear yourself think, tune out the hubbub with *Little Voice* and stop the insanity.

LV (Jane Horrocks)—short for Little Voice—hasn't said more than about two words since the passing of her sainted, and one assumes soft-spoken, father. Since then, her tarnished and more-than-just-presumably loudmouthed mother, Mari (Brenda Blethyn), and her ungovernable passions have drowned out LV's inner voice, and her outer one too. LV copes with the cacophony, probably much the way her father did—by listening to his vintage record collection over and over and over again. Through these grainy but melodic voices from a less loquacious past, and regular visits from her silent father's silent ghost, LV finds a voice of sorts to express her inner light.

Unfortunately, Little Voice is able to sing in anybody's voice but her own, literally. She develops an uncanny ability to impersonate the vocal stylings of such legends as Judy Garland and Marilyn Monroe. And when blowsy Mari's seedy, two-bit promoter boyfriend, Ray Say (Michael Caine), gets a load of LV's act, he wants to stick the whole dysfunctional drama under a spotlight, hang tassels on it, and take it on the road. But in the end he and LV and all of us learn that in order to find our inner light, sometimes we have to close our eyes and see; and to find our inner voice, sometimes we have to listen to the sounds of silence.

Get Off Your Cross, Someone Needs the Wood

When I'm not writing poems, I'm writing eulogies . . . mine.
★ Leelee Sobieski as Jennifer in *My First Mister*

There's nothing very special about me. I'm the kind of girl you usually don't notice: I scuttle in with a tray of tea, bow my head, and scuttle out.
★ Tara Fitzgerald as Betty in *The Englishman Who Went up a Hill but Came down a Mountain*

I'll be in my room, making no noise and pretending I don't exist.
★ Daniel Radcliffe as Harry Potter in *Harry Potter and the Chamber of Secrets*

▪ *Harry Potter and the Sorcerer's Stone* (2001)
Stars: Daniel Radcliffe, Rupert Grint, Emma Watson, Maggie Smith,
    Richard Harris, Alan Rickman
Director: Chris Columbus
Writer: Steven Kloves, based on the novel by J. K. Rowling

It's kind of difficult to let your light shine out when you're locked in a cupboard beneath the stairs, but as young Harry Potter learns, when you make the most of the opportunities presented to you and stay true to your principles and loyal to your friends, you too can become a dazzling and legendary wizard. And you may even inspire a multimedia empire with licensing rights that could finance the next seven generations.

When we first meet Harry (Daniel Radcliffe), he's completely unaware of his family legacy and totally unprepared for the reception he receives at boarding school—he's just relieved to get away from his cruel caretakers, the Dursleys. While the other students and teachers are either in awe of him or plotting his downfall, Harry simply tries to keep a low profile and hang out with fellow Gryffindor housemates Hermione Granger (Emma Watson) and Ron Weasley (Rupert Grint). But Harry discovers that you can't just brush your bangs over that lightning-shaped scar on your forehead and forget about your past forever. There are a lot of dark secrets in the shadows and evil forces that need to be subdued once and for all—and a lot of sequels to be made and toy store shelves to be filled. Yep, Harry better stop lurking in the corners and start harnessing the power of his resplendence.

Feeling like you're stuck in the cupboard and ready to claim your wand and your destiny? Let Harry Potter remind you of the importance of embracing who you are and where you came from—and developing your skills at manipulating the forces in your universe.

Until the juice ferments a while in the cask, it isn't wine. If you
wish your heart to be bright, you must do a little work.

—Rumi

▪ *The Eyes of Tammy Faye* (2000)
Stars: Tammy Faye Bakker, RuPaul
Directors: Fenton Bailey, Randy Barbato

The lights of the electric church never shined brighter than in the eyes of Tammy Faye Bakker, the terminally perky, perpetually double-lashed mistress of the Christian Broadcasting Network.

This documentary, narrated by RuPaul (who knows a thing or two about casting off bushels himself, even though the light underneath may make some squint), examines the indomitable spirit of the mother of televangelism whose unwavering beacon kept her on course, despite a sea of dysfunction, treachery, adultery, larceny, and public humiliation, not to mention the worst tattooed lip and eyeliner we've ever seen.

Tammy's personal and professional voyage is fraught with difficulty. She endures an unfaithful husband, a ruthless press, an addiction to prescription drugs, and the public's sudden and shocking disenchantment with puppetry as a central metaphor for the human condition. Tammy Faye's personal arc of the covenant ends up landlocked in Arizona, the home of the New Age movement, which is a dubious conclusion for a Christian morality tale. Yes, Tammy herself winds up literally in the desert, without a husband, a church, or most important, a satellite network or a theme park. Yet despite undergoing the trails and tribulations of Job, Tammy's light continues to shine through the darkness, with the same freakish but unwavering inner glow that is made of more than just Maybelline. And in the end, she is reborn to a new media career, a new agency contract, and a new husband.

So the next time you're feeling like your porch light is flickering, take a look at the world through *The Eyes of Tammy Faye*, and remember that what's important about shining out is what your light reveals to you, whether or not anyone else sees things the same way. Let Tammy Faye's all-day waterproof mascara inspire you not to give up on the brink of a miracle.

Tammy's Terrific Tidbits

*Yes. I have always loved lip liner! I like definition.
It makes my lips pop. I guess I like pop all over! I mean, why
blend it all in? If you're gonna blend everything in, why put it
on in the first place?*

★ Tammy Faye in *The Eyes of Tammy Faye*

You can't go forward looking in the rearview mirror.

★ Tammy Faye in *The Eyes of Tammy Faye*

*All in all, even if the film was not about me, I would want to take
time and go see it for the lessons it conveys. I think everyone,
especially young people, should see it and realize that there is
still life after tragedy and that the human spirit is strong and
resilient.*

★ Tammy Faye in *The Eyes of Tammy Faye*

■ **Devil's Playground** (2002)
*Stars: Faron Yoder, Velda Bontrager, Emma Miller,
Joann Hockstetler, Gerald Yutzy*
Director: Lucy Walker

If ever there were a group of people who needed to squint to find their inner light, it's the teenagers featured in this riveting documentary about the Amish tradition of *rumspringa*.

At age sixteen, all Amish kids enter *rumspringa*, a time when theoretically they get "vaccinated" against the outside world by having a small taste of the "English" (as the Amish call anything or anyone who isn't Amish) life before committing once and for all to baptism in the Amish church. In other words, children who have no more than eighth-grade educations, no personal connections outside of the community, and no handle on modern life or pop culture go mad crazy. Yeah, sure, exchanging clothing held together by straight pins for something with zippers is a part of it, but as this documentary shows, so are all-night crystal-meth-fueled raves.

Okay, so there is something admirable about a culture that acknowledges the need to indulge in a little hedonism and sow a few wild oats before settling in. But the contrast between Amish and "English" ways is so great, and the modern world so downright dangerous to an uneducated teen with few rules to rein him or her in and so little self-knowledge, that the consequences for these kids can be deadly. And since all of them are absolutely certain that hell is a real place, and that unbaptized, Kangol-cap-wearing, Tupac-wannabe, crank-dealing teenagers are headed straight to Satan's house, the "choice" of Amish security versus "English" uncertainty is pretty much a no-brainer. When some of the kids—particularly the girls, who have been thoroughly indoctrinated in patriarchal groupthink—actually walk away from everyone and everything they know and embrace an uncertain but hopeful future, it is a testament to their incredible character and resilience.

When you're feeling unsettled and unsure of what you really want, watch this documentary about kids who are far less equipped than you are to lift up that bushel and let the light shine out. See if it doesn't make you a little more confident—and a little more grateful for the insight, knowledge, and tools you do have.

Viewer's Note: Be sure to check out the extra features on the DVD to find out about the triumphs of two of the more courageous girls.

Maggie's Morsels

Safety does not come first. Goodness, truth, and beauty come first.

★ Maggie Smith as Miss Jean Brodie in
The Prime of Miss Jean Brodie

Oh, chrysanthemums. Such . . . serviceable flowers.

★ Maggie Smith as Miss Jean Brodie in
The Prime of Miss Jean Brodie

We'll leave you alone, but we'll be listening from the kitchen, so talk loud.

★ Maggie Smith as Caro Eliza Bennett in
Divine Secrets of the Ya-Ya Sisterhood

▪ *The Full Monty* (1997)
Stars: Robert Carlyle, Tom Wilkinson, Mark Addy, William Snape, Steve Huison
Director: Peter Cattaneo
Writer: Simon Beaufoy

In the northern England town of Sheffield, the steel mill has shut down and there's not much for a man to do except fill out his unemployment forms and show up regularly at the "job club" office to dully report that yes, he has actively looked for work and no, he hasn't found any hot prospects besides nicking a rusty steel beam from the old factory and selling it for scrap. Well, okay, Gaz (Robert Carlyle) doesn't actually report such shenanigans, but he really doesn't have any other ideas as to how he's going to pay his child support. Gaz is content to wander about town aimlessly, hanging out with his friend Dave (Mark Addy) and his son, Nathan (William Snape), until his ex-wife threatens to replace him utterly with a financially stable new husband who can slip neatly into the "dad" role.

Frightened of losing his son, and already stripped of his pride in being a working man, he decides that this is more emasculation than he can possibly bear. Then, inspired by a local troupe of male strippers who blow through town and depart with lots of money in their G-strings courtesy of the local females, Gaz comes up with a plan for reclaiming his pride and manhood. He rounds up several other ego-bruised men from the community and encourages them to accentuate the positive, stop focusing on the negative, and once again believe in themselves and their, er, formidable assets. All they need is a little encouragement from each other, a bit of rehearsal, and some faux-leather breakaway thongs, and they can conquer the world again.

When you're in need of a fun reminder that no matter what one's future prospects are, we all have something worth shaking on a Saturday night, check out *The Full Monty* and loosen up those lower chakras.

Words to Live By

It is not our abilities that tell us what we truly are . . . it is our choices.
★ Richard Harris as Dumbledore in
Harry Potter and the Chamber of Secrets

All I'm saying is, when we split the check three ways, the steak eater picks the pocket of the salad man.
★ Hank Azaria as the Blue Raja in *Mystery Men*

People don't like to have fire poked . . . POKED into their noses.
★ Christopher Guest as Corky St. Clair in *Waiting for Guffman*

The Sound of One Hand Clapping

Kids don't like eating at school, but if they have a **Remains of the Day** *lunchbox they're a lot happier.*

★ Christopher Guest as Corky St. Clair in *Waiting for Guffman*

The appearance of law must be maintained, especially when it's being broken.

★ Jim Broadbent as Boss Tweed in *Gangs of New York*

Nothing deranges a woman's mind more than marriage.

★ Ronald Colman as Professor Michael Lightcap in *The Talk of the Town*

■ *Ruthless People* (1986)
Stars: Bette Midler, Danny DeVito, Judge Reinhold, Bill Pullman, Helen Slater
Directors: Jim Abrahams, David Zucker
Writer: Dale Launer, based on the story "The Ransom of Red Chief" by O. Henry

Only the divine Miss M could find a way to let her light shine from inside a locked and sunless cupboard, buried in the bowels of somebody else's suburban basement. But as this eighties classic reminds us, sometimes it takes a few days alone in the dark to see the light.

Barbara Stone (Bette Midler) is taken hostage by two of the most meek and well-meaning criminals ever to pinch a diva. The kidnappers, Ken (Judge Reinhold) and Sandy (Helen Slater), get a lot more than they bargained for because Barbara Stone does not take naturally to hostagehood. Barbara is nobody's victim. Neither chains, nor blindfolds, nor threats of bodily harm can force her to mind her manners.

So it is no wonder that Sam Stone (Danny DeVito), Barbara's husband, would rather pay the kidnappers to lose his wife than return her. While Sam and the kidnappers engage in a bargain-basement battle over the price of Barbara's ransom, a strange thing happens down there in the dark. Barbara starts to glimpse her inner light. She begins, as many of us do, with a regular fitness routine, which she manages despite her manacles. She then convinces her kidnappers to be more conscientious about the fat grams in her food, and soon, Barbara Stone is no longer an evil-tempered and foul-mouthed, marked-down-for-clearance hostage anymore, but a hundred-watt diva whose brilliance illuminates everyone around her, even her kidnappers and her errant husband.

If you're feeling like your light has been buried somewhere underneath the boxes in the basement behind your old yearbooks and yesterday's bad fashion statements, let *Ruthless People* encourage you that all you have to do is open one little window to let the sun shine in and banish all that emotional damp rot.

Nancy's Momentous Minutiae: "Go Ahead and Stop Me"

Young Lucille Ball was thrown out of John Murray Anderson's Dramatic School because, they said, she was "too shy" to be an actress.

Sophia Loren's childhood nickname was "Toothpick."

The producer of the Marx Brothers' second film, *Cocoanuts*, informed Groucho that he couldn't step out of character and address the audience—it just wasn't done. And audiences would never tolerate that phony black painted-on mustache.

As a little girl, Nicole Kidman wanted a Barbie doll, but her feminist mother said absolutely no way—so Nicole stole one.

The notes on Fred Astaire's original audition for the movies read, "Can't sing. Can't act. Can dance a little."

Junk Food for the Soul

Crossroads (2002)
Stars: *Britney Spears, Zoe Saldana, Taryn Manning,*
    Anson Mount, Dan Ackroyd
Director: *Tamra Davis*
Writer: *Shonda Rhimes*

We are all for movies that celebrate girlfriends helping each other to discover their inner light and become independent women of substance who have something to offer the world. And this is exactly the kind of positive, empowering girl-friendly message that *Crossroads*, the latest addition to the Britney Spears industrial complex, purports to offer today's generation of not-girls-but-not-yet-women. Unfortunately, much like a lot of promises from the industrial complex, like thin thighs in thirty days, for example, what you see is not necessarily what you get.

Lucy (Britney Spears), class valedictorian and consummate good girl despite the startlingly convincing Madonna-style shimmy shake she does in her underwear in the first frame, graduates from high school filled with regret because although she got straight A's, she didn't get to go to any football games or parties. She longs to break free from her father's (Dan Ackroyd) authority and have fun. Lucy joins forces with childhood gal pals Kit (Zoe Saldana) and Mimi (Taryn Manning), and together they embark on a road trip in search of their collective womanhood.

Unfortunately, along the way Britney merely changes one form of patriarchy for another. No sooner does she find a little bit of independence than she trades it in for a personal and a professional collaboration with a disgruntled and paternalistic ex-con, Bev (Anson Mount), who is prone to

. . . *continued*

temper tantrums, doesn't like chick music, and has such severe control issues that he won't let anyone else hold the steering wheel. We wish that Britney, a role model for a new millennium, would have found a more interesting light at the end of her tunnel than nailing the chauffeur in the backseat of a vintage Chevy that she's not even allowed to drive.

All those wise men are like mariners on the deep: their wisdom confounded by the roaring seas.

—Psalm 5 of the Dead Sea Scrolls

Chapter 2

Like a Phoenix from the Ashes: Come On Up, We're Rising Movies

We don't like to face it, but we all know that it's true. As kind as the universe ultimately is, and as resilient as the human spirit can be, sometimes the rope snaps, the door closes, the fire goes out, the camel's back buckles, and the worst really does happen. When it does, and we're having a little trouble glimpsing the light at the end of the tunnel, it can be helpful to watch a movie that reminds us that it's always darkest just before the dawn and that we will survive to see the rescue boats arrive in the morning. So while you're waiting for your morning after, console yourself with one of these Come On Up, We're Rising Movies, about eagles and angels whose wings have been scorched but not broken, who manage to soar out of the ashes, back toward the sun.

■ *Frida* (2002)
Stars: *Salma Hayek, Alfred Molina, Edward Norton*
Director: *Julie Taymor*
Writers: *Clancy Sigal, Diane Lake, Gregory Nava, Anna Thomas,*
    based on the book by Hayden Herrera

Pain, whether it's physical or emotional, can wear away at you until you feel downright crippled, but here's a movie that shows that when you use that pain creatively, you can not only rise above your suffering, but fashion a refreshingly different life and a lasting legacy.

Mexican painter Frida Kahlo (Salma Hayek) was barely a teenager when a trolley car accident changed her from a spirited perpetual motion machine to a woman who would spend her life in chronic physical pain. Stuck in a body cast for long stretches, she begins to draw and paint, creating beauty out of her suffering. She also fashions a bohemian life that breaks all the rules, and takes the risk of marrying famed muralist Diego Rivera (Alfred Molina), a self-confessed philanderer. Repression and discretion are requirements in their dynamic, so when a Ricki Lake–esque plot twist comes to the surface, Frida has a whole nother type of pain to deal with.

Well, it's true, any woman who requests that her husband offer her "not fidelity, but loyalty" is, in a sense, making her own bed. But if Frida's got to lie in it, she's going to put aside her physical and emotional pain and make damn sure that bed is carried crosstown to that one-woman art show she's finally earned for herself, so that her utterly fabulous self can greet her many admirers.

This is a great movie to watch when you feel that your choices are limited by your body, your gender, your background, or your heartbreak. So let go of your sorrows, pour yourself some tequila shots, watch *Frida*, and celebrate your own palette of possibilities.

> *Seek for the wine that opens the heart, ever more sparkling,*
>   *brightly new!*
>
> — *"The Song of Hafiz"*

The Real Nitty-Gritty

*Look, I have to go identify our dead father's body. I'm sorry you're
having a bad drug experience, but deal with it.*

★ Peter Krause as Nate Fisher in *Six Feet Under*

*I know stealing a foot is weird. But living in a house where a foot
is available is weird too.*

★ Lauren Ambrose as Claire Fisher in *Six Feet Under*

Tracy (Dina Spibey): Why do people have to die?
Nate (Peter Krause): To make life important.

★ from *Six Feet Under*

■ *Six Feet Under, Season 1* (2001)
  Stars: Peter Krause, Michael C. Hall, Frances Conroy,
    Lauren Ambrose, Rachel Griffiths
  Creator: Alan Ball

This series was created by the man who brought us *American Beauty*, so it is no surprise
that the first season focuses on the way in which the proximity to death can illuminate and
enhance our daily lives.

Nobody knows more about grief management than the Fisher family, owners of a funeral parlor, who are therefore obviously well equipped to handle tragedy when it comes
calling. The premiere episode finds the Fishers experiencing a sudden loss of their own,
when the patriarch of the family is killed in an automobile accident. Family members find
their lives frozen for an instant in time; they are forced to take stock of where they are,
where they've been, and where they're headed. The rest of the series follows them as they

try to rise from the ashes of their loss and find their way to a better and more fulfilling life. Intermingled with the Fishers' story each week are the stories of other families going through the rite of passage called death. Each episode begins with a death, moves through the stages of grief and guilt and strange relief that can accompany loss, and shows us how tragedy can enhance our appreciation for life here and now. Each episode brings us safely to a better place, on the other side of sadness, with a new understanding of the beauty and fragility of life.

Men Behaving Well

Honey, when you smile, it's like the sun comin' up.
★ Clark Gable as Gay Langland in *The Misfits*

All I know is, on the day your plane was to leave, if I had the power, I would turn the winds around, I would roll in the fog, I would bring in storms, I would change the polarity of the earth so compasses couldn't work, so your plane couldn't take off.
★ Steve Martin as Harris K. Telemacher in *L.A. Story*

Do you want to dance, or do you want to dance?
★ Pierce Brosnan as Thomas Crown in *The Thomas Crown Affair*

I love you and I think you're the greatest thing since spice racks. And I'd be knocked out several times if I could just have that first kiss, and I won't be distant. I'll come back in the morning. And I'll call you . . . if you let me.
★ Robin Williams as Parry in *The Fisher King*

■ *Country* (1984)

Stars: Jessica Lange, Sam Shepard, Matt Clark, Wilford Brimley
Director: Richard Pearce
Writer: William D. Wittliff

Sometimes the biggest threats to our security come out of the blue and from the least expected place, and we discover the hard way that while we can bend in the wind like wheat, some of the people we love snap like sticks under the strain. *Country* shows that even when it looks like you're completely beaten, the will to survive nurtures the seeds of triumph—and that hell hath no fury like a farm wife with a thirty-day foreclosure notice.

Jewell Ivy (Jessica Lange) and family have been surviving years of diminishing profits, tornadoes, and freak accidents, but nothing has prepared them for some pencil pusher with a proclamation that it's time for banks to stop being sentimental about family farms and call in all outstanding loans. Tom (Matt Clark), who works for the Feds, doesn't have much interest in considering the effect of years of drought and declining profits caused by government controls on grain exports. He just wants the farmers to auction off everything from their plows to their antique horse bridles and get the heck out of the way of "progress." But Jewell, deeply upset that her family and neighbors are falling apart under the strain, learns that about 40 percent of the farmers in the state are on his "close 'em up and move 'em out" list. Suddenly, she realizes that together they can at least kick up enough of a fuss so that their way of life won't disappear like so much topsoil in a dust storm.

When you're at a low point and feeling under pressure to roll over and admit defeat, watch *Country* and keep repeating, "We shall overcome."

My heart has no desire to stay/Where doubts arise and fears dismay/Though some may dwell where these abound,/My prayer, my aim, is higher ground.

—from the hymn "I'm Pressing on the Upward Way"

Just a-Talkin' to the Man Upstairs

*Congratulations on earth. It's a most excellent
planet, and Bill and I enjoy it on a daily
basis.*

★ Keanu Reeves as Ted, speaking to
God in *Bill and Ted's Bogus Journey*

*Oh Lord, bless this thy hand grenade that with it thou mayest
blow thy enemies to tiny bits . . . in thy mercy.*

★ St. "Attila" in Armaments 2:9–21,
as quoted by Brother Maynard's
roommate (Michael Palin) in
Monty Python and the Holy Grail

*Catherine, I'm afraid you'll have to ask the blessing. The Lord
knows I'm not grateful for turkey hash, and I can't fool him.*

★ Richard Todd as Rev. Peter Marshall
in *A Man Called Peter*

*No, nothing I ever do is good enough. Not beautiful enough.
It's not funny enough, it's not deep enough, it's not anything
enough. Now, when I see a rose, that's perfect. I mean, that's
perfect. I want to look up to God and say, "How the hell did
you do that? And why the hell can't I do that?"*

★ Roy Scheider as Joe Gideon
in *All That Jazz*

Cast Not Your Pearls Before Swine

Newspaperman: Mr. Roark, we're alone here.
Why don't you tell me what you think of me,
in any words you wish?
Roark (Gary Cooper): But I don't think of you.

★   from *The Fountainhead*

■ *Philadelphia* (1993)
  Stars: *Tom Hanks, Denzel Washington, Jason Robards, Mary Steenburgen*
  Director: *Jonathan Demme*
  Writer: *Ron Nyswaner*

Tom Hanks stars in the true story of Andrew Beckett, a gay man with AIDS working in an old-boy firm located in the very top knot of starched white-collar Philadelphia. Andrew is the apple of his old-boy, friendly-so-long-as-you're-not-gay boss Charles Wheeler's (Jason Robards) eye. Andrew can look forward to a powerful and lucrative career under Charlie's wing, as long as Wheeler never gets wind of who his golden boy actually is.

When Andrew develops KS lesions on his face and he's no longer able to hide his serostatus from the firm, he is peremptorily fired and forcibly removed from the premises. He is left to wander the streets of Philadelphia to a plaintive Bruce Springsteen ballad, suffering from AIDS in an age before protease inhibitors, without a job, without insurance, and ironically, without a lawyer, because no one will represent him in a suit against the most powerful firm in Philadelphia.

Yet even in the face of such certain defeat, Andrew fights back and joins forces with Joe Miller (Denzel Washington), a vaguely homophobic ambulance chaser whose life is illuminated by the sun inside of Andrew that refuses to go gently into that good night.

When you're up against insurmountable odds, let this real-life story about a hero who faces adversity with courage, grace, good humor, and a love for his fellow man remind you that when you find the strength to stand up and follow your path again, you'll never walk alone.

■ *The Misfits* (1960)
Stars: Marilyn Monroe, Clark Gable, Montgomery Clift, Thelma Ritter, Eli Wallach
Director: John Huston
Writer: Arthur Miller

Generally, a movie with lots of close-ups of Marilyn Monroe's wiggling derriere, directed by a real guy's guy, is not where you expect to find a moving story about a woman coming to terms with the losses in her life and fully feeling her difficult emotions regardless of how inconvenient they are for the men around her. But surprise—*The Misfits* isn't just about the difficulty of having a cowboy spirit in modern-day America. It's about how acceptance allows us to heal while stubborn denial turns us into anachronistic icons with a rapidly diminishing range to roam.

Marilyn Monroe plays Roslyn, a young woman who has come to Nevada to divorce her husband because she's decided that if she's going to be lonely she'd rather be lonely on her own than with him. Her new friend and landlady, Isabelle Steers (Thelma Ritter), warns her about keeping company with cowboys, which is understandable once we see that the cowboys in this movie can't face their pain unless they get sloppy drunk on whiskey. Roslyn, however, is a free spirit attracted to other free spirits, so she begins hanging out with not one, not two, but three cowboys (Eli Wallach, Clark Gable, and Montgomery Clift), all of whom think she's a beautiful beacon of innocence, joy, and child-woman sensuality. Well, that's because they willfully ignore her palpable sadness and penchant for tossing out cynical observations about trust, human nature, and the inevitability of suffering.

Eventually, however, the men's obstinate insistence on clinging to their past illusions at any cost and stomping out any spark of vulnerability culminate in an ill-advised mission to capture some wild mustangs to kill and sell for dog food. And despite Roslyn's proclivity for incorporating white furry stoles into her casual daywear wardrobe, this outrageous animal cruelty and obvious metaphor for denial and self-loathing makes her boil over with rage and recognize her own need to embrace life instead of death and truth instead of lies. Meanwhile, the cowboys have to decide to face up to their reality or keep trying to rope a dream that has disappeared along with the herds.

This is a great movie to watch when you're feeling like a misfit, stuck out on the range, waiting for some cowboy to ease your loneliness and give your life some purpose. It'll encourage you to saddle up your own horse, face the long journey ahead, and be willing to ride off into the sunset alone.

Words to Live By

Honey, we all got to go sometime, reason or no reason. Dyin's as natural as livin'. The man who's too afraid to die is too afraid to live.
★ Clark Gable as Gay Langland in *The Misfits*

Men should be explorers, no matter how old they are.
★ Don Ameche as Art Selwyn in *Cocoon*

God's given me a gift. I shovel well. I shovel very well.
★ William H. Macy as The Shoveler in *Mystery Men*

Be excellent to each other. . . . And party on, dudes!
★ Robert V. Barron as Abraham Lincoln in *Bill and Ted's Excellent Adventure*

▪ *Sounder* (1972)
Stars: Cicely Tyson, Paul Winfield, Kevin Hooks, Taj Mahal
Director: Martin Ritt
Writer: Lonne Elder III, based on the novel by William H. Armstrong

Face it: If you're stuck in the Deep South in 1933 and trying to make ends meet by sharecropping and coon hunting for the occasional source of protein, you're gonna want Cicely Tyson holding down the home front. Yes, the opening credits have hardly finished rolling when her husband, Nathan (Paul Winfield), is hauled off for having stolen a ham from the neighbors. Rebecca and her three children, led by the oldest, David Lee (Kevin Hooks), are left to fend for themselves. Between doing laundry for the neighbors, growing and picking cotton in the hot sun while covered with a perpetual layer of sweat, hauling the family around in a rickety wooden cart pulled by a mule, and holding back her anger when faced with redneck racism, Rebecca keeps herself very, very busy. Even so, when her eldest gets a chance for a quality education, she is determined to find a way to do without that extra pair of hands so that at least one member of her family can rise above this hardscrabble life.

This is one of those feel-good, triumphant movies about folks with simple lives and simple dreams. Watch it when you need an infusion of good old-fashioned optimism to get you through your own hard times.

❧

Oh don't you want to go to that gospel feast/That promised land/where all is peace?

—from the American spiritual "Deep River"

❧

▪ *The Pianist* (2002)

Stars: *Adrien Brody, Thomas Kretschmann, Frank Finlay, Michal Zebrowski*
Director: *Roman Polanski*
Writer: *Ronald Harwood, based on the memoir* Death of a City
  by Wladyslaw Szpilman

In this grim, violent, but ultimately uplifting movie based on a true story, pianist Wladyslaw Szpilman (Adrien Brody) has the extremely bad fortune of being a Jew in Poland in 1939. And he doesn't realize that despite his levelheaded, sensible approach to life, he's about to experience a grotesque absurdity that has all the makings of an epic statement on what it means to be human.

Szpilman is the type of fellow who *should* survive under the worst circumstances: coolheaded enough to avoid fruitless confrontations, clever enough to find creative solutions to a never-ending parade of disasters, and savvy enough to understand that a little ego stroking applied to the right petty official at the right time can mean the difference between doom and survival. Unfortunately, in the Warsaw ghetto, all bets are off: As Szpilman witnesses one atrocity after another, each one more shocking than the last, he comes to comprehend that fate can be as ridiculous as it is arbitrary. For some unfathomable reason, he keeps waking up in the morning, alive. Given what's going on around him, this is the equivalent of winning Powerball and being struck by lightning at the same moment. All he can do is make the most of his serendipity one day and run for his life the next.

What keeps him in touch with his humanity and identity in the black hole of Warsaw during World War II is hearing a snippet of a piano sonata on a radio or a verse of Shakespeare that's unnervingly apropos to the situation. Ultimately, it's his ability to create music that helps him rise out of his lonely isolation and find a connection to the heart of a person who has the power to destroy him but instead chooses to give him bread, a warm coat, and a can opener—which, when you're down to nothing but a tiny hiding space and an industrial-size can of okra, is a survival tool of the highest order.

Watch this one when you're feeling like your world is just one ludicrous little debacle after another, and be reminded that embracing art in any form reconnects us to others as well as to our own souls, and enables us to do more than just survive—it allows us to live.

Reel to Real

The real Szpilman not only made it through World War II but lived to age eighty-eight, becoming a popular and prolific composer and pianist.

Nancy's Momentous Minutiae: "We Are Not Amused"

Charlie Chaplin spoofed Hitler in *The Great Dictator*, a movie that he began filming in 1937 (it was released in 1940) but later said had he known just how evil Hitler and the Nazis were he wouldn't have been able to find the humor in their madness. Hardly amused by Chaplin's depiction of him goose-stepping, Hitler banned the movie in Germany—but secretly got ahold of it and watched it twice.

What's New, Pussycat? (1965) was banned in Norway because of the scene where Peter Sellers's character tries to commit suicide by wrapping himself up in a Norwegian flag and setting himself on fire.

The Producers (1968) was banned in Germany because of that classic song-and-dance number "Springtime for Hitler." It was eventually shown as part of a film festival celebrating the works of Jewish moviemakers.

The Marx Brothers' spoof on a fascist dictator, *Duck Soup* (1933), so incensed Benito Mussolini that he banned the film in Italy—which, naturally, delighted the Marx Brothers.

- *Antwone Fisher* (2002)
  Stars: Derek Luke, Denzel Washington, Joy Bryant
  Director: Denzel Washington
  Writer: Antwone Fisher

Antwone Fisher (Derek Luke) has one nasty temper, which constantly gets him in trouble with his employer, the U.S. Navy. Their quick-fix solution to his deeply rooted anger, abandonment, and father issues is three sessions with a psychiatrist. Given that Antwone spends the first two and a half sessions in stony silence, resolving his inner conflicts seems about as likely an outcome as getting low-cost supplemental health insurance coverage for two sessions a week indefinitely.

Luckily for Antwone, Dr. Jerome Davenport (Denzel Washington) finds himself drawn to the young man and keeps encouraging him to bring to the surface all the pain he's been repressing. And it's a mother lode of pain that makes you wonder how he managed to survive at all. Mere survival, however, is not enough in Dr. Davenport's book, so he urges Antwone to make peace with his past, and though Antwone resists at first, he is encouraged by the kind support of Davenport and his wife, and his new girlfriend, Cheryl (Joy Bryant). Antwone at last bravely marches up to the house of horrors from his past, lets himself in, and starts doing the hard work that will allow him to reclaim the love he deserves.

This isn't just a feel-good story, it's a full-out cathartic weeper about hope, healing, and the human spirit that'll inspire you to believe that you too can find the courage to face up to your fears and reinvent yourself and your life. Watch it when you're feeling particularly pessimistic about your future and dismissive of the significance of confronting your past and see if it doesn't make you believe that you too can rise above.

He who is slow to anger is better than the mighty; and he who rules his spirit is better than he who conquers a city.

—Prov. 16:32

Reel to Real

Antwone Fisher was working as a security guard at Sony Pictures when he took a screenwriting course and wrote a draft of a screenplay telling his life story. He refused to sell the story rights, certain that somehow his own screenplay could be filmed. Eventually, he succeeded in getting it to Denzel Washington, who got the movie made.

Bev's Culinarytherapy: The Sun Will Come Out Tomorrow Pancakes

The next time you're feeling like you're under a dark cloud, whip up a batch of these pancakes and look on the sunny side.

Here's what you'll need:

> 1 butternut squash
> 1 teaspoon nutmeg
> 3 tablespoons butter
> 1 tablespoon maple syrup, plus extra for topping
> salt
> 1 box of your favorite pancake mix
> 2 tablespoons powdered sugar
> whipped cream, if desired

. . . continued

Here's how you do it:

Peel the squash using a vegetable peeler. Cut it in half, seed, and slice it into thin wedges. Place in a sauté pan, cover with water, and simmer for about 15 minutes until the squash is soft. Drain and puree, adding a little nutmeg, maple syrup, and salt. Set aside. Make pancakes with pancake mix following the instructions on the box, but substitute 1 cup pureed squash for 1 cup of the required liquid, and add the powdered sugar to the mix. Coat griddle with butter and cook pancakes about 2 minutes on each side or until they're golden brown. Serve with maple syrup and/or whipped cream.

■ *Rabbit-Proof Fence* (2002)

Stars: Everlyn Sampi, Laura Monaghan, Tianna Sansbury, Kenneth Branagh, Ningali Lawford, Myarn Lawford, David Gulpilil

Director: Phillip Noyce

Writer: Christine Olsen, based on the book Follow the Rabbit-Proof Fence by Doris Pilkington

If ever there was a movie that will inspire your inner child to believe that whatever your challenges, you can reconnect with the source of your strength, *Rabbit-Proof Fence* is it. After all, your journey home probably won't demand of you a fifteen-hundred-mile, nine-week trek on foot across the Australian bush. Or weeks in the desert with only the blistering sun to guide you. Or having to carry an eight-year-old on your back while you pick your way through stones and brambles.

It's hard to believe this is a true story, but back in 1931 a half-white, half-Aboriginal girl named Molly (Everlyn Sampi) decided to take a pass on the Australian government's racist plans for her future. Molly, you see, was wrenched from her mother (Ningali Lawford) and grandmother (Myarn Lawford) to be raised in a boarding school designed to teach her and other young "half-castes" to meet their inherent potential—which the local government official, Mr. Neville (Kenneth Branagh), defines as being a domestic servant to white farmers. This is not exactly Molly's vision of personal fulfillment. She's fourteen and she wants to go home to her mother, thank you very much, so she, along with her eight-year-old sister, Daisy (Tianna Sansbury), and her cousin, Gracie (Laura Monaghan), take off in nothing but cotton dresses and Keds toward their home in the bush halfway across the continent.

Molly's a few steps ahead of your typical Girl Scout. She doesn't need a compass, a mess kit, or a backpack full of food and water, thanks to the hunting and tracking skills her mother and grandmother taught her. She knows where she belongs, and Molly is downright certain that even the Aboriginal tracker (David Gulpilil) hired by the boarding school will never capture her, and that ultimately she will be in charge of her own destiny.

Feeling that the forces of other people's expectations and the difficulties of the journey will prevent you from making it to the place in your life where you really want to be? Watch *Rabbit-Proof Fence* and be awed by the power of determination. We'll bet that you'll feel a lot more confident about your own provisions, sense of direction, and willpower.

❧

Train up a child in the way he should go, and even when he is old, he will not depart from it.

—Prov. 22:6

❧

Junk Food for the Soul

How Green Was My Valley (1941)
Stars: *Roddy McDowall, Donald Crisp,*
    Maureen O'Hara, Walter Pidgeon, Sara Allgood
Director: *John Ford*
Writer: *Philip Dunne, based on the novel*
    by Richard Llewellyn

Yes, the Welsh choir's voices are stirring. Yes, Roddy McDowall's big sad eyes always make our own misty, especially when he's stricken by one of those mysterious movie illnesses that renders him a whispering invalid for a year because he caught a chill. And yes, Maureen O'Hara always looks like some goddess of the British Isles taking human form. And we really do hate to pick on a classic family film by one of the cinema's greatest directors. But it's hard to feel sentimental about how verdant that valley used to be, with its flocks of sheep ambling through the lanes and the proudly earned streaks of coal on the miners' skin, when we know that most of these men lived grimly short lives thanks to horrendous accidents and fatal lung ailments.

We'd probably have felt a lot better about this movie had the hopeful young preacher (Walter Pidgeon) not sat silent as a single mother was cruelly cast out of the community's church. Or had the big sister of the family (Maureen O'Hara) been liberated from scrubbing buckets and not ended up a lonely, unhappy widow. Or had little Huw Morgan (Roddy McDowall) decided to be the hope of his village and embraced a future as an educated man instead of choosing to fit in with his family and work in the mines, despite overwhelming evidence that it's a dying industry that'll ruin his health before chewing him up and spitting him out.

. . . *continued*

Hey, we're all for optimism, but we find that movies that don't acknowledge that misery exists are never quite as enriching or uplifting as movies that don't confuse optimism with a total denial of reality. Somehow, the honesty in the dark-humored *Margaret's Museum* (1995)—a far less sentimental movie about the grim plight of miners in the British Isles—touched our spirits more than this treacly flick.

▪ *The Wizard of Oz* (1939)
Stars: Judy Garland, Frank Morgan, Ray Bolger, Bert Lahr, Jack Haley,
  Billie Burke
Directors: Victor Fleming, Richard Thorpe
Writers: Noel Langley, Florence Ryerson, Edgar Allan Woolf,
  based on the novel The Wonderful Wizard of Oz *by L. Frank Baum*

There's not much we can do to hold back the forces of nature, whether they be little dogs that are compelled to chase the nasty neighbor's cat or tornadoes whirling across the plains of Kansas. But as *The Wizard of Oz* shows, sometimes we overlook our abilities and underestimate our powers and find ourselves traveling crooked paths through dark woods in search of some all-powerful being who will give us all the answers and solve all our problems. Like Dorothy Gale (Judy Garland), we don't realize that we have the power within ourselves to go back to our source of strength and joy anytime we choose to tap our heels. Like the scarecrow, the tin man, and the lion, we look outside ourselves for confirmation of our wisdom, our goodness, and our courage. But the secret revealed at the end of this classic fairy tale is not only that our wizards are usually just fearful men with a lot of smoke and mirrors and projections, but that if we're ever going to make it out of that sleepy poppy field and get to where we want to go, we've got to acknowledge our own power.

Now, it's true that when we're caught up in that land of color, magic, and song it's a little hard to understand why Dorothy is so anxious to get back to that bleak gray farm so quickly. Couldn't she hang out with the Lullaby League a little longer and learn to toe-dance? Or indulge in a few more spa days in the Emerald City? Then again, anyone's nirvana might look a little pale and plain to someone else. So we say, when you're feeling caught up in a whirlwind that's disconnected you from your source, make no apologies, pop in *The Wizard of Oz*, and enjoy the journey back home to where your heart is.

&

Though clouds may gather in the sky/And billows 'round me roll/However dark the world may be/I've sunlight in my soul.
—from the hymn "I Wandered in the Shades of Night"

&

Chapter 3

Side by Side:
Finding Your Soul Mate Movies

Are you exhausted from searching the world over for your other half? Are you beginning to wonder if yours is the only soul in the universe that wasn't created as a part of a matched pair? Well, relax. We don't live in a twin-set world anymore. We have options. Today, prints are going with plaids, florals are hanging out with solids, and no one even thinks twice about blending polka dots with stripes.

So the next time you're feeling like a left without a right, watch one of these Finding Your Soul Mate Movies about people who have opened themselves up to new possibilities, learned to mix and match, and found happiness as coordinated separates.

▪ *Iris* (2001)
 Stars: Kate Winslet, Judi Dench, Jim Broadbent
 Director: Richard Eyre
 Writers: Richard Eyre, Charles Wood, based on the books
   Iris: A Memoir *and* Elegy for Iris *by John Bayley*

So often when Hollywood imagines two soul mates finding one another, they present us with bucolic images of young and supple-limbed lovers strolling along a beach or through a meadow, or tooling through the old-world charm of some Continental capital or another on a moped while "That's Amore" crescendos in the background. This can make it hard for us mere mortal and somewhat less than supple lovers to recognize a good thing when it comes along. Because as we all know, true love is not always a Kodak moment.

Iris is a biopic of Iris Murdoch (Judi Dench and Kate Winslet), a passionate and brilliant novelist and philosopher whose bright spirit was overshadowed by Alzheimer's disease at the end of her life. Accompanying her through her spirited youth, then through her creative prime, and finally on the long sail into darkness of her later life, is her soul mate and husband, John Bayley (Jim Broadbent). John's unwavering concern for, appreciation of, and even anger toward his soul mate as she moves in and out of lucidity is one of the most compelling and three-dimensional depictions of the love and devotion that can exist between soul mates ever presented on the silver screen. This is not a fairy tale with a neatly crafted "happily ever after" at the conclusion. But John Bayley, and all of us who experience this last phase of a brilliant life, learn that a soul mate is as simple but as essential and irreplaceable as someone who shares your memories and laughs at your jokes.

▪ *My Big Fat Greek Wedding* (2002)
 Stars: Nia Vardalos, John Corbett, Lainie Kazan, Michael Constantine, Andrea Martin
 Director: Joel Zwick
 Writer: Nia Vardalos, based on her one-woman stage show

It's tempting to think that once we find true love we will never again have to admit to being that goofy-looking little kid whose mom made her brown-bag moussaka when everyone else ate Wonder Bread sandwiches. But as this movie reminds us, if we want to embrace our soul mate we've got to embrace our past and our whole selves. And really, isn't it easier to just fess up about your crazy family and your dweeby tendencies than try to keep a lid on all those nutty people dancing the Miserlou on your lawn?

Thirty-year-old Fortoula "Toula" Portokalos (Nia Vardalos) has a very Greek father who expects her to carry on the family's female legacy of marrying a nice Greek man, bearing lots of Greek babies, and consuming way too many Greek carbs. With help from her mother and aunt, Toula hopes to break the intergenerational pattern of breeding and baking to excess. We're happy to report that the life makeover she's itching for starts not with a typical Hollywood Rodeo Drive shopping montage, but the way so many real-life makeovers start—with college classes that open her mind and help her find her voice.

At this point, it's only natural that true love—in the form of the twinkly-eyed and sensual John Corbett—shows up. Soon Toula realizes she wants to create a new family with him, but it's going to take a lot of compromise, honest talks, and ouzo consumption to bring it all together. Only then can Toula feel optimistic that her big fat Greek wedding will lead to a big fat happily-ever-after that she has scripted herself.

Watch this one when you're ready to face the dork side, and be reassured that when you do, your soul mate will embrace it as fully as you do.

 ## Nia's Nut Creams

When I was growing up, I knew I was different. The other girls were blond and delicate, and I was a swarthy six-year-old with sideburns.
★   Nia Vardalos as Toula in *My Big Fat Greek Wedding*

I had to go to Greek school, where I sat in a room translating, "If Nick has one goat and Maria has nine, how soon will they marry?"
★   Nia Vardalos as Toula in *My Big Fat Greek Wedding*

❧

*Joyful the moment when we sat in the bower, Thou and I; In two forms
and with two faces—with one soul, Thou and I.* ❧ Rumi

❧

■ *You've Got Mail* (1998)
Stars: Meg Ryan, Tom Hanks, Greg Kinnear, Parker Posey
Director: Nora Ephron
Writers: Nora Ephron, Delia Ephron, based on the play Parfumerie *by Miklós László*

If you've been keeping the lights burning late in the window of your little shop around the corner but no one's buying, and you're beginning to think it might be time to shut the doors and call it a day, this movie might be just what you need to stave off that emotional liquidation sale and keep yourself in business.

Independent bookstore owner Kathleen Kelly (Meg Ryan) struggles to keep her shop alive when a rival superstore tycoon, Joe Fox (Tom Hanks), comes to her neighborhood intent on driving her out of business. To make matters worse, Kathleen is adrift in her personal life, dating a man she doesn't love and wondering if she will ever find her soul mate and live happily ever after.

Kathleen's only consolation is an e-mail correspondence she guiltily indulges in with a man that she's never met. When she discovers that her cyberprince is none other than rival bookstore king Joe Fox, Kathleen learns that there's a lot more to that old adage about loving your enemy than they teach you in Sunday school. This movie is a great reminder that love doesn't always ride into our lives on a white horse with a big sign that reads MADE FOR YOU. But if we are open to love, regardless of its origins, then even an enemy can become a soul mate.

👀 *So Nice They Made It Twice:* The 1940 version with James Stewart and Margaret Sullavan, called *The Shop Around the Corner*, features some spirited performances, but too many scenes take place on fake-looking sets, which can't quite compare to *You've Got Mail*'s love affair with New York City.

Cheese and Crackers

Well, I'm kind of a nice guy, and you're a very lovely girl, so whaddya say, would you like to take a shower?

    ★ Chevy Chase as Tony Carlson in *Foul Play*

Your eyes are amazing, do you know that? You should never shut them, not even at night.

    ★ Olivier Martinez as Paul Martel in *Unfaithful*

I don't mean to toot my own horn, but if Jesus Christ lived in Chicago today, and he had five thousand dollars, let's just say things would have turned out differently.

    ★ Richard Gere as lawyer Billy Flynn in *Chicago*

You must've torn out the "Q" section in my dictionary, because I don't know the meaning of the word "quit"!

    ★ Ben Stiller as Mr. Furious in *Mystery Men*

Tell me, did you write the song "I'll never smile again"?

    ★ Cary Grant as Nickie Ferrante in *An Affair to Remember*

I'm back, my love. . . . I went to make a garland of beach plums to place atop your glorious head like a crown. But then I caught sight of that sunset and . . . I don't know . . . something stirred inside me and I had to stop and cry.

    ★ Brendan Fraser as Elliot in *Bedazzled*

▪ *The Black Stallion* (1979)

Stars: Kelly Reno, Teri Garr, Mickey Rooney, Hoyt Axton
Director: Carroll Ballard
Writers: Melissa Mathison, Jeanne Rosenberg, William D. Wittliff,
   based on the novel by Walter Farley

The Black Stallion is a quietly beautiful portrayal of love and friendship between a kid and a horse who meet, fall in love, and discover freedom in interdependence.

It's the 1940s and the ship Alec Ramsey (Kelly Reno) is traveling on with his father (Hoyt Axton) catches fire and sinks. The next morning Alec finds himself on an island with a huge, scary wild black stallion that survived as well. The two of them have no other companions, not even a volleyball named Wilson. And though it was mistreated by its handlers, this horse has an elephant's memory: It hasn't forgotten how Alec gave him sugar cubes and helped free him from ropes when they fell overboard. Oh, the Black (as Alex dubs him) is still skittish, but among the turquoise lagoons, tranquil tide pools, and vast expanses of untrodden sand, horse and boy begin a dance of intimacy—first tentative, then exuberant, then playful. Finally, as the sun begins to set, they fall into an easy comfort.

Eventually, however, boy and horse are rescued and have to adjust to a more structured world, where horses don't run freely and little boys don't ride wild stallions without their mothers' official permission. It takes an old man named Henry (Mickey Rooney) to help the boy and the black stallion to once again cut loose and fly forward with passion and freedom, knowing that they have each other.

Even if you're not "horsey," if you've ever felt a spiritual connection to an animal that's not just a pet but a familiar, this movie will speak straight to your heart. So snuggle up with your furry one—or feathered or scaly one—and celebrate your bond.

∽

A *faithful friend* is the medicine of life.

—Ecclesiastes 6:16

∽

Nancy's Momentous Minutiae:
Me and My Familiar

Actress Liz Taylor loved her adorable four Pekingese lapdogs, but when the British told her she couldn't bring them into the country unless she quarantined them, she kenneled them instead . . . in a $2,500-a-week rented yacht that was anchored offshore.

Drew Barrymore and Tom Green were saved from a fire when their Labrador-Chow mix, Flossie, did a turn as Lassie and woke them up in the nick of time.

Doris Day, Tippi Hedren, and Brigitte Bardot all retired from acting and became animal advocates, starting their own foundations.

What's Love Got to Do with It?

Sure I love Goldie. How could you not love Goldie? Everyone loves Goldie. I love her, and I hope our love will continue, but I don't want to give an I-love-Goldie-Hawn interview.

★ Kurt Russell

I've only been in love with a beer bottle and a mirror.

★ Sid Vicious

My wife heard me say I love you a thousand times, but she never once heard me say sorry.

★ Bruce Willis

Junk Food for the Soul

Maid in Manhattan (2002)
Stars: Jennifer Lopez, Ralph Fiennes
Director: Wayne Wang
Writer: Kevin Wade, based on a story by John Hughes

This is one of those modern romantic comedies that tries to be politically correct and show that love can conquer all, and that a working-class Hispanic single mom from the South Bronx and a well-manicured white Republican politician can become soul mates. And yet, despite the optimistically nonpartisan pairing of hotel maid Marisa Ventura (Jennifer Lopez) with senatorial candidate Christopher Marshall (Ralph Fiennes), Chris doesn't even notice Marisa when she's just another maid in a uniform. No, she has to go on a *Pretty Woman*–esque shopping spree and play Cinderella to win the heart of the prince, because apparently he's only aware of women when they're in designer duds. But he is a prince, of course, a real catch because he . . . because he . . . well, because he's rich, of course.

All right, so Chris is nice to Marisa's kid. And he promises to look into the problems of the Hispanic community that she mentions—that is, if his handlers can fit a trip to the South Bronx into his busy, busy schedule. But we find it sad that all the rich plot potential between two people from very different worlds gets discarded in favor of a romantic cliché like a man falling in love with a pretty girl because she wears an expensive, tastefully subdued evening gown and seems to be something she's not—a wealthy society woman. Frankly, we would've liked to see Marisa show up at that hoity-toity party in one of those J. Lo "Here's my backside, love it or leave it" cut-down-to-there power dresses. Somehow, we just find it more romantic when the gal gets to stay real no matter how much money she has, celebrate her own uniqueness, and attract an equally iconoclastic fellow with assets that are emotional, not financial.

■ *Amélie* (2001)

Stars: Audrey Tatou, Mathieu Kassovitz
Director: Jean-Pierre Jeunet
Writer: Guillaume Laurant, based on a story by Guillaume Laurant
and Jean-Pierre Jeunet

The eccentric Amélie (Audrey Tatou) certainly has a reason for shying away from an intimate relationship: Her overprotective parents have raised their daughter to fear sudden heart failure. Isolated in her home by her parents, Amélie befriends only one creature: Blubber the goldfish. And even he becomes suicidal over life in a tiny bowl and repeatedly tries to flop his way out of despair and into the great beyond. This doesn't exactly provide a hopeful metaphor for Amélie, nor does it help when her mother is accidentally killed by a suicidal tourist who jumps off Notre Dame cathedral and lands on the poor woman's head. No wonder Amélie feels that fate is a powerful force not to be trusted.

Rather than sink into a nihilistic funk, however, she learns to take joy in the simple things, like sinking her hand into a sack of grain or cracking crème brûlée with a teaspoon. Amélie also begins constructing a rich internal life to ease her loneliness. And as she grows up, she brings small joys into the lives of the people she meets in her own quiet, whimsical way. But will Amélie find the courage to express her own inner longings, reach out for love and intimacy, and leave behind her fantasy world? Will she finally connect with Nino (Mathieu Kassovitz), a man who appreciates her quirkiness? Will Amélie have to wait for a happy accident, or will the love that she has generated come back to her with all its power and joy and absurdity?

This is a delightful movie to watch when you're secretly hesitant to expand your circle of love to include that one special someone. It'll inspire you to embrace your quirks, trust in the karma, and put some of that Lady Bountiful effort into going after what you deserve.

Soul Sisters

Because there is nothing like a best girlfriend to remind us that we're not alone.

Beaches (1988)
Stars: Bette Midler, Barbara Hershey
Director: Garry Marshall
Writer: Mary Agnes Donoghue, based on the novel Forever Friends
   by Iris Rainer Dart

When you're feeling like you've been grounded on the tarmac of life, there's nothing like reconnecting with your best girlfriend to help you rediscover your lift and thrust, and fly the friendly skies with the wind of sisterhood beneath your wings.

CC (Bette Midler) and Hillary (Barbara Hershey) meet as children on vacation in Atlantic City. From the moment they meet they are fascinated with each other, perhaps because they are as different as chalk and cheese. Hillary is a privileged child from the locked jaw of New England. Everything about her screams out Ivy League breeding and future Harvard Law School grad. And CC is, well, she's Bette Midler. Although life leads them in different directions both personally and geographically, and they have a few considerable spats, they remain touchstones for each other through thick and thin.

Romy and Michelle's High School Reunion (1997)
Stars: Lisa Kudrow, Mira Sorvino, Janeane Garofalo, Alan Cumming
Director: David Mirkin
Writer: Robin Schiff, based on her play The Ladies' Room

When you're feeling like the odd woman out at the high school reunion of life, this movie reminds you that any woman can be the queen of the prom, as long as she's got a soul mate she can rely on. Romy (Mira Sorvino) and Michelle (Lisa Kudrow) are two imaginatively accessorized soul mates who take stock of their lives on the cusp of their ten-year high school reunion and realize that they don't really add up to much. So they launch a personal revolution and storm the citadel of their own potential. What they discover, however, is that success doesn't lie in a better career or ten fewer pounds, but in just being such good friends that even folding scarves is heaven, because they're folding them together.

The Banger Sisters (2002)
Stars: Goldie Hawn, Susan Sarandon, Geoffrey Rush
Director and Writer: Bob Dolman

Suzette (Goldie Hawn) and Lavinia (Susan Sarandon) are former groupie girlfriends who drifted apart once the Jefferson Airplane reached its final destination. Now, years later, Lavinia is the respectable wife of a respectable attorney in a respectable mansion in the respectable part of town. Suzette, on the other hand, is a middle-aged version of Hawn's own daughter's role in *Almost Famous,* which is a whole other kettle of fish, but you get the picture. Suzette rocks on while Lavinia has lost her mojo. That is, until Suzette shows up, pulls Lavinia out of her PTA meeting, and sets her inner wild child free once more. Watch this one when you and your soul sisters need to get back in touch with your inner rock star, and rave on.

Bette Bites

But enough about me, let's talk about you . . . what do you think of me?

★ Bette Midler as CC Bloom in *Beaches*

I hate men who smell like beer and bean dip . . . and makin' love in the back of recreational vehicles!

★ Bette Midler as Sadie Ratliff in *Big Business*

My Morty becomes this big shot on TV. He was selling electronics, right? On our twentieth wedding anniversary he hits midlife crisis major. He starts working out, he, he grows a mustache, he gets an earring. I said, "Morty, Morty, what are you? A pirate? What's next? A parrot?" And all of a sudden I'm a big drag. I'm holding him back because I won't go roller-blading.

★ Bette Midler as Brenda in *First Wives Club*

▪ *The Odd Couple* (1968)

Stars: Jack Lemmon, Walter Matthau
Director: Gene Saks
Writer: Neil Simon

They love each other, they really do. Although Felix Ungar (Jack Lemmon) has a penchant for cream cheese and pimiento on date nut bread and Oscar Madison (Walter Matthau) serves brown sandwiches and green ones (very new cheese or very old meat, he's not sure which), these poker partners are friends for life. So when Felix is thrown out of the house by his beloved wife—who probably has had enough of his histrionics, perfectionism, and moose-call sinus clearings—Oscar takes him in. After all, Oscar's got eight rooms and is late with his alimony payments.

At first, opposites attract and the two of them have the best of both worlds—an immaculate apartment and perfectly cooked meals courtesy of Felix, and a couple of swinging gals looking for a few laughs, courtesy of Oscar. Felix is grateful for his friend's generosity and Oscar accepts Felix despite his neuroses—"You're you. You walk and talk and cry and complain and eat little green pills and send suicide telegrams—no one else does that," he tells him. But like many friends before and many friends after, Felix and Oscar come to realize that mutual respect and admiration are a lot easier to maintain when you've got your own space. Can this marriage be saved? Can they reach a truce and negotiate a demilitarized zone and protocol that will hold them together for a weekly half-hour show with syndication potential?

If you and someone you care for are in need of Jimmy Carter and a week at Camp David, why not have a laugh together at *The Odd Couple* and be reassured that your loving bond can survive anything, even being roommates.

∽

He that harpeth on a matter estrangeth a familiar friend.

—Prov. 17:9

∽

▪ *Elizabeth* (1998)
  Stars: Cate Blanchett, Geoffrey Rush, Joseph Fiennes
  Director: Shekhar Kapur
  Writer: Michael Hirst

Sometimes a soul mate isn't another person at all, but a country. This stunning biopic of the incomparable Liz the First is a perfect example of the golden age that can ensue when the soul of a great woman, and the soul of a great cause, meet and marry.

Elizabeth (Cate Blanchett) comes to power in a bitterly divided, not to mention financially challenged, England. Elizabeth, a young girl more interested in Lord Dudley's codpiece than affairs of state, is ripped out of the bucolic innocence of her maidenhood and transported to the tower for execution at the hands of her Catholic half-sister, Mary. Then, just as suddenly, she is crowned queen of England. Unfortunately, this also makes Elizabeth a target for every zealous Catholic with an ax to grind, as well as every royal eligible European bachelor with a crown complex. No one expects her to survive.

Elizabeth's advisers inform her that her only security lies in marriage, but Elizabeth only has eyes for Lord Dudley. But when even Lord Dudley and his codpiece conspire against her, Elizabeth hears and heeds the call of her true soul mate, rejects all suitors, and marries her true compatriot, England. She rules, a mistress with no master, over a golden age for forty years, and is remembered as the Virgin Queen who loved only her people. Watch this movie when you need a reminder that sometimes a soul mate is not a person at all, but a cause worth living and dying for.

Men Who Really Are from Mars

Everyone's a dick in high school, Vince. It's the white male, football playing prerogative. The trick is to evolve into something else once you're out.

★ Robert Sean Leonard as Jon in *Tape*

When you can balance a tack hammer on your head, you can head off your foes with a balanced attack.

★ Wes Studi as The Sphinx in *Mystery Men*

Women Who Really Are from Venus

I'm cooking a brisket for dinner tonight. A woman needs to eat blood every now and again. She just really does. ★ Carol Kane in *My First Mister*

. . . continued

Relationships are not fair. They're battles, battles for supremacy.
★ Tovah Feldshuh in *Happy Accidents*

The men may be the head of the house but the women are the neck and they can turn the head any way they want.
★ Lainie Kazan as Maria Portokalos in *My Big Fat Greek Wedding*

■ *The Agony and the Ecstasy* (1965)
Stars: Charlton Heston, Rex Harrison, Diane Cilento
Director: Carol Reed
Writers: Irving Stone, Philip Dunne, based on the novel by Irving Stone

Feeling compelled to engage with your nemesis, but find yourself grudgingly admiring him? Here's a movie that'll convince you that your love/hate relationship just might turn into a love/love connection that enriches both of you—and those around you.

Michelangelo (Charlton Heston) has been a renowned sculptor since age fifteen when he first began to probe the potentialities of a block of marble, bringing forth its inner light and making it glow like alabaster. And he's got a day job he's perfectly content with: designing and creating forty massive sculptures to glorify the tomb of Pope Julius II (Rex Harrison). Okay, so it'll take about 140 years to complete his plans—he's an artist, not a numbers cruncher.

But the pope has something else in mind for the famed artist from Florence: a painting job. On a ceiling of his favorite little chapel, the Sistine. Michelangelo is totally uninterested, but in fifteenth-century Italy you just didn't say "No, thanks, I'm booked" to the pope. So he agrees to the commission, then proceeds to grumble, moan, throw hissy fits, and storm off in a huff, only to be dragged back by the royal police. The pope, for his part, doesn't deliver on his promises to pay Michelangelo—probably because he has done renovations before and recognizes that rule number one is to hold on to your checkbook until the job's done.

And given Michelangelo's questionable talents at doing accurate estimates, the pope knows he could be dethroned, dead, and buried before the scaffolding can come down.

Yet somehow, for all their bickering, bargaining, psychological manipulations, and differences in vision, deep down these two ambitious men understand that they need each other to complete an astonishing work of art that will stand as a legacy to faith, love, and determination; a labor of love reflective of what two people can do when they set aside their differences and devote their energies to something larger than themselves.

So if a certain someone keeps getting under your skin and yet you secretly suspect he's the best thing that's happened to you in a long time, pop in *The Agony and the Ecstasy* and see if it doesn't make you appreciate and cherish your soul connection.

Viewer's Note: You'll have to be patient through a twelve-minute prologue and a lengthy battle scene to get into the meat of the movie.

Cell Mates

Maximum security makes for some strange soul fellows . . .

Kiss of the Spider Woman (1985)
Stars: *William Hurt, Raul Julia, Sonia Braga*
Director: *Hector Babenco*
Writer: *Leonard Schrader, based on the novel by Manuel Puig*

We admit that a smoldering Latin revolutionary who wears his machismo slung around his waist like a gun belt, and a lyrical preop transsexual who wears his prison blues like a silk kimono don't exactly sound like a match made in heaven. And a few years' hard time locked together in a three-by-nine cell in a Mexican prison don't exactly sound like a dream date. But that is exactly what evolves when Luis (William Hurt) begins to tell his tale and captures Valentin (Raul Julia) in a web of fantasy that carries both men away to a happier world where pain, injustice, and gender boundaries have no meaning, and where they are wrapped in the warm blanket of Luis's imagination and his love for his cell mate.

The Silence of the Lambs (1991)
Stars: Jodie Foster, Anthony Hopkins, Scott Glenn, Ted Levine
Director: Jonathan Demme
Writer: Ted Tally, based on the novel by Thomas Harris

Fledgling FBI agent Clarice Starling (Jodie Foster) and elegant cannibal Hannibal Lecter (Anthony Hopkins) are one of the most intriguing pairs of disparate yet strangely kindred spirits ever drawn. Clarice must unlock the secrets of this psychiatrist-turned-serial-killer's elegant but lethal soul, but in exchange, she must reveal her own. Is this a cat-and-mouse game between an interrogator and her prisoner, or the twisted dance of two soul mates struggling to reach through the bars? We're not sure, but Clarice and her cannibal suggest that the soul has a few appetites that are best not fed.

The Interview (1998)
Stars: Hugo Weaving, Tony Martin
Director: Craig Monahan
Writers: Craig Monahan, Gordon Davie

Mild-mannered, just-your-average-Aussie-guy Eddie (Hugo Weaving) is raided by police while asleep in his bed in the middle of the night. He's taken at gunpoint to an interrogation room and left to sweat and wonder at this strange turn of events.

At last Detective John Steele (Tony Martin), his interrogator, arrives and what ensues is an intricate chess match between two souls who must look to each other for redemption, and they leave us all wondering who is guilty and who is innocent. This movie reminds us that sometimes we come across soul mates whom we may not like, but who seem to have been put in our path to teach our soul a lesson.

Ruth's Rum Balls

Reach out. Take a chance. Get hurt, even! Play as well as you can. Go team! Go! Give me an L! Give me an I! Give me a V! Give me an E! L. I. V. E. Live! . . . Otherwise, you got nothing to talk about in the locker room.

★ Ruth Gordon as Maude in *Harold and Maude*

Vice, virtue, it's best not to be too moral—you cheat yourself out of too much life. Aim above morality.

★ Ruth Gordon as Maude in *Harold and Maude*

Pray? No, I communicate.

★ Ruth Gordon as Maude in *Harold and Maude*

■ *Harold and Maude* (1971)
Stars: Bud Cort, Ruth Gordon
Director: Hal Ashby
Writer: Colin Higgins

Sometimes soul mates turn up in the darnedest places. And never was there a more unlikely cosmic coupling than Harold and Maude: a poor little rich boy with a death wish and a seventy-nine-year-old Holocaust survivor with an unquenchable thirst for life. Harold (Bud Cort), an adolescent malcontent who is obsessed with the ultimate futility of all human endeavor, spends his days eluding his mother's attempts to marry him off to the nearest heiress, staging mock suicide attempts, attending the funerals of strangers, and avoiding life. It is at one such funeral that he first spies Maude (Ruth Gordon), a mischievous septuagenarian standing amid a sea of anonymous mourners, with an impish grin on her face. When Maude suddenly breaks from the crowd and pinches the priest's car, Harold instantly recognizes a partner in crime, and together they hit the "road to find out." They discover the thrill of risk, the wisdom of nature, the comfort of companionship, and the joy of living.

This is a great movie to watch when you're beginning to lose faith that you'll ever find a companion on the road trip toward your destiny. *Harold and Maude* reminds us that when the student is ready, the teacher appears, and that it is never too late for love as long as you remain open to life in all of its infinite variety.

Chapter 4

The Buck Stops Here: Accepting Personal Responsibility Movies

Has your ax gotten too big to fit on the grinder? Has that chip on your shoulder moved to your lower lumbar region and is now threatening to break the camel's back? Let's face it, we can all wind up feeling a little overburdened from time to time. And no matter how much we do, no matter how far we go out of our way, nobody seems to appreciate it.

If you're tired of going hungry at the all-you-can-eat buffet of life and you're ready to climb down off that cross and demand your fair share, take control with one of these Accepting Personal Responsibility Movies about heroes and heroines who take responsibility for their own nourishment, or learn the hard way about the high cost of having to sing for their supper.

■ *Unfaithful* (2002)

Stars: Diane Lane, Richard Gere, Olivier Martinez
Director: Adrian Lyne
Writers: Claude Chabrol, Alvin Sargent

On the surface, Connie Sumner (Diane Lane) has it all: a beautiful house, a bright child, and a doting, understanding, and successful husband (Richard Gere) who still looks pretty damn good with his shirt off. And as if that's not enough, she still looks great in a halter dress. Who could ask for anything more? Well, the French could, of course!

This Claude Chabrol–inspired thriller pits pleasure against responsibility in a post-existential world where the only absolute truth is the obligation to enjoy yourself as long as you can live with the consequences. When enjoying yourself involves doing a last tango in Paris with a Gallic Brad Pitt called Paul (Olivier Martinez), however, the potential for moral paradox becomes clear. For no sooner does the dawn break on Connie's Lawrencian sensual reawakening than her husband begins to see the light, and the sun begins to set on this Lady Chatterley's lover.

So if you've been hungering for a diversion and are considering dabbling in the discreet charms of the bourgeoisie, let *Unfaithful* remind you that you'd better make sure you can pay the bill of fare, or you could wind up washing dishes in the karmic kitchen of the universe for the rest of your life.

■ *The Others* (2001)

Stars: Nicole Kidman, Fionnula Flanagan, Alakina Mann, James Bentley
Director and Writer: Alejandro Amenábar

This movie plays like a feature-length commercial for psychotherapy and reminds us all of the way in which the past can haunt the present until we open the drapes of our denial and face the consequences of our actions in the full light of day.

Grace Stewart (Nicole Kidman) lives alone with her two children, Anne (Alakina Mann) and Nicholas (James Bentley), in a house that looks like it's straight out of a

Hitchcock movie, poised on the cliff of some metaphorical sea or another—a house just begging for somebody to walk in and reveal the intrigue that is so obviously concealed there. Which is probably why there are such strict rules in the house, all of which the children as well as the household staff must follow to the letter, and all of which have obvious Freudian implications that will no doubt come home to roost sometime in the future should they make a sequel. For example, you can't open a door until you have shut the one you have just come through; you're not allowed to run; and never under any circumstances are you to ever shed any light on the situation . . . EVER.

When strange and uninvited apparitions begin to haunt the house, showing complete disregard for all of its careful rules, however, it becomes impossible for Grace to keep her secrets, or her photosensitive children, in the dark any longer.

Watch this one when you've been avoiding the obvious, and let Grace encourage you to face facts before you become a ghost haunting your own life. Grace teaches us that the first step in assuming personal responsibility is acknowledging the way things are, rather than how we wish they were, and acting in accordance with reality rather than our own frustrated expectations.

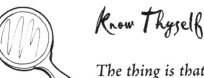

Know Thyself

The thing is that a person's life is like a TV show.
I was the star of **The Will Show** *and* **The**
Will Show *is not an ensemble drama.*
> ★ Hugh Grant as Will in *About a Boy*

I've been sober too long, Margaret; it's kept me from thinking straight.
> ★ Kenneth Welsh as Angus MacNeil in *Margaret's Museum*

I'm just a little tense. This whole office is not Feng Shui. All the
desks are facing evil.
> ★ Sean Whalen as Merkin in *Never Been Kissed*

■ *The Fisher King* (1991)
Stars: Robin Williams, Jeff Bridges, Amanda Plummer, Mercedes Ruehl
Director: Terry Gilliam
Writer: Richard LaGravanese

There's exactly one line in the planned sitcom based on his life that Howard Stern-esque shock jock Jack Lucas (Jeff Bridges) can't deliver with sincerity: "Forgive me." And it's no wonder: Jack spends his days sealed off in an airtight, sterile little room where he can say whatever he likes, broadcasting his words into the great unknown, without spending a moment thinking about the consequences. And then one day the grim fallout from a careless remark destroys Jack's career. Left bitter, aimless, utterly dependent on a golden-hearted girlfriend (Mercedes Ruehl) with a soft spot for lost dogs like Jack—and without the lead role in a lucrative sitcom—Jack falls into a funk.

Then one night in the midst of a drunken binge, Jack runs into a bizarre homeless man, Parry (Robin Williams), who lives somewhere underneath the sidewalks and is seeking the Holy Grail. Funny, but this grail bears a striking resemblance to a child's spelling bee trophy and is owned by some rich guy living in a castlelike home on Fifth Avenue.

Now, Jack may not recognize an allusion to British mythology about redemption when it smacks him upside the head, nor does it occur to him that he's got a subconscious reason for carrying around that Pinocchio doll he somehow acquired. But Jack does have the goodness of heart to seize the opportunity to make up for his past deeds and become a "real boy" and heal his own mortal wounds. Can he unite Parry with the woman he desires (Amanda Plummer) and capture the grail, making himself whole again in the process?

When you've been wronged, *The Fisher King* will keep you laughing even as it reassures you that even the most hardened and unrepentant cynic can come around to making amends.

If a Tree Falls in the Forest . . .

There is no such thing as a mistake. There are things you do, and things you don't do.
★ Olivier Martinez as Paul in *Unfaithful*

The fact that you stopped it from falling doesn't mean it wasn't going to fall. ★ Tom Cruise as John Anderton in *Minority Report*

You know your own future, which means you can change it if you want to. ★ Tom Cruise as John Anderton in *Minority Report*

■ *Minority Report* (2002)
Stars: Tom Cruise, Max von Sydow
Director: Steven Spielberg
Writer: Scott Frank, Jon Cohen, based on the short story by Philip K. Dick

There's nothing like a big-screen epic about free will versus determinism to put you back in the driver's seat of your own destiny. This futuristic thriller stars Tom Cruise as Detective John Anderton, the head of a crack unit of police who use "precogs" who can see into the future to predict precrimes that Anderton and his force can then prevent. When the precogs point their finger at Anderton himself, however, what results is an existential race against Anderton's own foregone conclusion, which features a whole bunch of really great chase scenes, as well as a very important philosophical question: If we know our future, can we do anything to change it? Can we really choose our reality? And as *Minority Report* clearly illustrates, the answer to that question is a resounding yes. Watch this movie when you're feeling inclined to stick your head in the sand, and let John Anderton remind you that knowing is always better than not knowing, and that the only way to change your tomorrow is to accept personal responsibility for determining your own destiny.

Junk Food for the Soul

I Am Sam (2001)
Stars: *Sean Penn, Michelle Pfeiffer, Dianne Wiest,*
    Dakota Fanning, Loretta Devine, Richard Schiff
Director: *Jessie Nelson*
Writers: *Kristine Johnson, Jessie Nelson*

We're not sure when it became PC to laugh at the mentally handicapped as if they were adorable little kids who say the darnedest things, but we get the distinct sense that we're not supposed to be spoilsports and ask pointed questions about this film. In fact, this whole movie is so overly sentimentalized it's like a Thomas Kinkade painting with the promise of a cozy cottage filled with love and light that'll distract you from all of life's harsh realities. But somehow, we couldn't help wondering, just how does a single parent who is mentally disabled manage to raise a child from newborn to the age of seven with no help from social services or nondisabled adults? Simple: The kindly agoraphobic next-door neighbor (Dianne Wiest) pops by the first day to offer full-time, year-round child care, unpaid. Pretty darned convenient.

Somehow, she must have been there to keep up on vaccination schedules and well-baby visits, baby-proofing the apartment, toilet training, and toddler discipline. Funny how no doctor ever questioned Sam's (Sean Penn) ability to parent his daughter (Dakota Fanning) before she became old enough to spout platitudes like "All you need is love" on cue. But then this is a movie that expects us to scorn those "evil" social services people (Loretta Devine, Richard Schiff) because they dare to question whether Sam's love for his daughter is all he needs to make him a terrific parent. Boo! Hiss! Didn't Sam figure out how to use his answering machine with a little help from his (also mentally disabled) friends?

. . . continued

Hey, we can be suckers for soft-focus father/daughter love montages at the playground to the soundtrack of classic Beatles songs, just like anyone else. But in real life, bumper-sticker slogans and poignant moments on the swing set are no substitute for genuine social services or true unconditional love that allows a parent to admit he needs a heaping amount of practical support to genuinely do right by the child he loves.

■ *A Place in the Sun* (1951)

Stars: Montgomery Clift, Elizabeth Taylor, Shelley Winters
Director: George Stevens
Writers: Michael Wilson, Harry Brown, based on the play by Patrick Kearney,
based on the novel An American Tragedy *by Theodore Dreiser*

Naturally, we all want to find a sunny spot in which to lay down and bask in our blessings, but the path to that spot can present a lot of tempting side trails, and ultimately the failure to commit to one road or another can leave us wandering in the woods. Or split in half from trying to travel in two directions at once. Or frantically concocting an alibi for a really poorly-thought-out crime of passion.

George Eastman (Montgomery Clift) comes from the poorer branch of a wealthy family and is willing to work his way up from a lowly job at his uncle's factory. But before long, George falls madly in love with an unattainable princess (Elizabeth Taylor, who else?) and gets caught between a spirited, exquisite society girl with an eye for him and a needy, vulnerable, yet sexually available factory worker who loves him desperately (Shelley Winters). Money or sex? Privilege or privileges? Understandably, George wants to have it both ways, but the laws of biology and the rage of a woman scorned and experiencing telltale morning sickness demand that he make some hard choices.

Luckily, most of us have a lot more paths open to us than George and his girlfriends, and we can even tamp down a few weeds and make new ones if we're brave enough. But even when we're not happy with our limited range of choices, sometimes we still have to buck up and pick one, just one. *A Place in the Sun* is a good reminder that it's not so easy to double back and start over, so perhaps you'd better research all your options carefully lest you become your own American tragedy.

⌇

Like a steel mirror, scour off all rust with contrition.　　　　—Rumi

⌇

■ *In the Bedroom* (2001)
　Stars: Sissy Spacek, Tom Wilkinson, Nick Stahl, Marisa Tomei
　Director: Todd Field
　Writers: Robert Festinger, Todd Field, based on the short story "Killings"
　　by André Dubus

In the Bedroom is a sobering reminder of what can happen when well-mannered and civilized people come face-to-face with violence and refuse to do anything about it because they don't want to rock the boat.

All-American boy Frank Fowler (Nick Stahl) falls in love with Natalie (Marisa Tomei), the divorcée down the street with two kids, a troubled past, and an abusive ex-husband who hangs around and busts up birthday parties, threatens violence, and just generally makes a big fat hairy nuisance of himself. Frank's mom, Ruth (Sissy Spacek), a controlling choir director with high hopes for her son, urges Frank to be responsible and keep his mind on school. But Frank's dad, Matt (Tom Wilkinson), who recognizes a good time when he sees her and is used to allowing his son license to compensate for his wife's short leash, encourages Frank to follow his heart. When Natalie's ex-husband begins to explode, what we are left with is two parents who are so busy holding the other responsible that they can't take responsibility themselves, an abuser who won't take responsibility for his anger, a battered woman who won't take responsibility for her bad choices, and a promising young man who must pay the price for them all. When you've been walking on eggshells and afraid to call a spade a spade because you don't want to hurt anybody's feelings, let this movie remind you that it's better to make waves than to drown.

Nancy's Momentous Minutiae: Sleeping Soundly at Night

A refrigerator was the original time-traveling machine in *Back to the Future*, but director Robert Zemeckis and executive producer Steven Spielberg were afraid it might give children the idea to crawl into refrigerators, so they used a car as the time-traveling device instead.

Each time Richard Widmark had to deliver racist lines to fellow actor Sidney Poitier in *No Way Out* (1950), he apologized to him.

Having played the part of Paul, the soldier who learns about the ultimate futility and dehumanizing effects of war in the grim *All Quiet on the Western Front* (1930), was one of the reasons Lew Ayres petitioned for and received conscientious objector status in World War II. His action prompted more than one hundred Chicago movie houses to ban his films.

James Stewart's father was none too pleased with the seedy story in *Anatomy of a Murder*, and felt it was his obligation to place an ad in a newspaper pleading with the public not to patronize his son's "dirty picture."

■ *The Rookie* (2002)
Stars: Dennis Quaid, Rachel Griffiths, Beth Grant, Brian Cox
Director: John Lee Hancock
Writer: Mike Rich, based on the true story of Jim Morris

We all have dreams that we eventually realized weren't going to work out. But what if, through some freakish twist of fate, we had a second chance to live them?

Jim Morris (Dennis Quaid) claims that really, it's no big deal that he never got to pitch a major-league baseball game even though he spent every waking hour of his childhood practicing. Yep, status quo is just fine by him, and regrets would have nothing to do with why he hasn't seen or called Dad (Brian Cox) since who knows when. (Hey, this is a baseball movie—you were expecting a healthy and resolved father/son relationship?)

Jim prefers not to think about what could've been had he not blown out his pitching arm. Stuck in the desert somewhere in Texas, coaching high school baseball in a land of cactus, oil wells, and football fanatics, Jim just wants to be a responsible husband and father. But to his shock, he discovers that his arm has healed in such a way that when he pitches—*whoop, thwap!*—the radar registers ninety-five miles an hour, which means he could actually try out for the majors again. Jim is unnerved because he thinks that being an adult means never having to say, "Honey, I'm not sure where my next paycheck is coming from."

It takes a supportive wife (Rachel Griffiths), a wise mother who has come to terms with her own disappointments (Beth Grant), and some surprisingly mature high schoolers to challenge Jim to consider that maybe we all have a responsibility to nurture our talents—and that we owe it to our kids to be role models who courageously pursue our hearts' desires.

The Rookie is a great movie to watch when you find yourself boxed in by thoughts of what you "should" do. We think it'll open you up to the possibility that taking risks is an important part of being a stable and responsible grown-up.

Promises, Promises

I can teach you how to bewitch the mind, and ensnare the senses.
I can teach you how to bottle fame, brew glory, and even put a
stopper on death.
    ★ Alan Rickman as Snape in *Harry Potter and the Sorcerer's Stone*

We've got armadillos in our trousers. It's really quite frightening.
    ★ Christopher Guest as Nigel Tufnel in *This Is Spinal Tap*

With God on Our Side

What better place to set a morality tale than in the hallowed halls of the military, where the first rule is to follow the orders of your superiors, and personal responsibility is often set aside in the name of God and country? These movies remind us that no matter what your rank or file, one day all soldiers for the cause will have to take responsibility for their actions, with no one at their side but their own consciences.

The General's Daughter (1999)
Stars: John Travolta, Madeleine Stowe, James Cromwell, Timothy Hutton
Director: Simon West
Writers: Christopher Bertolini, William Goldman, based on the novel
    by Nelson DeMille

When Lieutenant General Joseph Campbell's (James Cromwell) daughter Sara (Madeleine Stowe) is found staked out and strangled to death on the base where her father is commander, it is up to Warrant Officer Paul Brenner (John Travolta) to serve the warrant on the responsible party. Brenner follows the paper trail to the door of the general, who is left holding the bag at last for a buck he passed many years ago in the service of the corps, and at the expense of his daughter. When you're feeling like closing your eyes and pulling the covers over your head instead of facing the music, let *The General's Daughter* remind you that just because you refuse to look at something doesn't mean it will go away.

A Few Good Men (1992)
Stars: Tom Cruise, Jack Nicholson, Demi Moore, Kevin Bacon,
    Kiefer Sutherland
Director: Rob Reiner
Writer: Aaron Sorkin, based on his play

When Private Santiago is rubbed out for "breaking the code" and two of his fellow marines are arrested for the murder, it is up to Lieutenant

. . . continued

Daniel Kaffee (Tom Cruise) to pull apart the rank and file and find out who is really responsible. Standing in the way is big man on base, Colonel Jessep (Jack Nicholson), who waves his authority like a flag on the high wall between us and the enemy, and dares us to question him. Fortunately for democracy, Kaffee has no respect for authority, and demands that Jessep finally take responsibility for the lives he has sacrificed in the name of God and country.

When you're in the mood to question your orders, but you're worried that you'll risk a full frontal attack, let *A Few Good Men* remind you that the only solidarity you really need is to be able to stand face-to-face with your own conscience.

Apocalypse Now (1979)
Stars: Martin Sheen, Robert Duvall, Marlon Brando, Dennis Hopper
Director: Francis Ford Coppola
Writers: John Milius, Francis Ford Coppola, narration written by
Michael Herr, based on the novel Heart of Darkness *by*
Joseph Conrad

This classic seventies war-is-hell epic, featuring one of those freakish cameos by Marlon Brando so characteristic of the era, is perhaps one of the most visceral—and certainly one of the most cardiovascular—illustrations of the horrors of war ever filmed during a monsoon in Malaysia. Capt. Ben Willard (Martin Sheen) is sent to relieve special ops Colonel Kurtz (Marlon Brando), who has transformed himself from a war hero into a freaked-out jungle demigod in a strictly Dionysian sense of the word, and must be brought home to pasture. The only trouble is, Captain Willard has to find him first, and as he approaches the heart of Kurtz's darkness, he must confront the ecological disaster that can occur when a big fish is left in a small pond, with no one around to challenge him on the food chain. Watch this movie when you're questioning your pecking order, and remember that might isn't always right.

Them's Fightin' Words

Son, we live in a world that has walls, and those walls have to be guarded by men with guns.

★ Jack Nicholson as Colonel Jessep in *A Few Good Men*

You have to have men who are moral . . . and at the same time who are able to utilize their primordial instincts to kill without feeling . . . without passion . . . without judgment . . . without judgment. Because it's judgment that defeats us.

★ Marlon Brando as Colonel Kurtz in *Apocalypse Now*

Hey, man, you don't talk to the colonel. You listen to him. The man's enlarged my mind. He's a poet-warrior in the classic sense. I mean sometimes he'll, uh, well, you'll say hello to him, right? And he'll just walk right by you, and he won't even notice you. And suddenly he'll grab you, and he'll throw you in a corner, and he'll say do you know that "if" is the middle word in life? If you can keep your head when all about you are losing theirs and blaming it on you, if you can trust yourself when all men doubt you—I mean I'm no, I can't—I'm a little man, I'm a little man, he's, he's a great man. I should have been a pair of ragged claws scuttling across floors of silent seas.

★ Dennis Hopper as the photojournalist in *Apocalypse Now*

You smell that? Do you smell that? . . . Napalm, son. Nothing else in the world smells like that. I love the smell of napalm in the morning.

★ Robert Duvall as Lieutenant Colonel Kilgore in *Apocalypse Now*

Know Thyself

I'm a man in search of his true self. How archetypically American can you get? We're all trying to fulfill ourselves, understand ourselves, get in touch with ourselves, face the reality of ourselves, explore ourselves, expand ourselves. Ever since we dispensed with God we've got nothing but ourselves to explain this meaningless horror of life.

★ William Hurt as Eddie Jessup in *Altered States*

■ *Catch Me If You Can* (2002)
Stars: Leonardo DiCaprio, Tom Hanks, Christopher Walken, Nathalie Baye
Director: Steven Spielberg
Writer: Jeff Nathanson, based on the book by Frank Abagnale Jr. and Stan Redding

It's tempting to try to fix the problems of the people we love who have always been our support system. But in general, if you find yourself frantically trying to resurrect your parents' failed marriage and rescue your father from the consequences of tax evasion, you might want to consider whether kiting some checks so that you hand your pop the keys to his very own midlife-crisis-red Cadillac is truly the best use of your talents, skills, and determination . . . and whether any of this is gonna bring Mom back when she's already got a new boyfriend.

But Frank Abagnale (Leonardo DiCaprio) is a can-do kind of kid with a stack of blank checks for his modest bank account, a brilliant mind, an astonishing ability to hold it together under pressure, and plenty of adolescent illusions about his power to fix what is irretrievably broken. Hence, he begins a career of bank fraud that's one for the record books, and starts masquerading as an airline pilot because, after all, no one questions a handsome young man with wings on his shoulder. And the uniforms look really snappy.

Before long, a clever and fiercely determined FBI investigator, Carl Hanratty (Tom Hanks), is on Abagnale's trail. Alas, he's no match for the charismatic and ingenious Abagnale. What's really going to bring the kid down in the end is the fact that all of those beautiful stewardesses, condo pool parties, and Italian wool sweaters just aren't adding up to any sort of internal peace for him, and Mom and Dad just aren't going along with his plan for redemption. What's a boy to do?

When you've been running away from changes that were inevitable, watch *Catch Me If You Can* and remember that operating out of fear instead of embracing an uncertain future is never a good idea. And the surprise ending will have you thinking about the great ironies you can create by wasting your energy trying to micromanage your world instead of being responsible for yourself.

Though the Way is quite broad, people love shortcuts.

—Tao Te Ching

▪ *School Ties* (1992)
Stars: Brendan Fraser, Matt Damon, Ben Affleck, Chris O'Donnell
Director: Robert Mandel
Writers: Dick Wolf, Darryl Ponicsan, based on a story by Dick Wolf

Teenage football star David Greene (Brendan Fraser) is an honest kid, but in his eagerness to be worthy of the fancy East Coast prep school scholarship that has been bestowed upon him, he finds that the pressure to hide his true self is like having an entire defensive line pile up on his head. At first David, who has been warned in no uncertain terms to keep mum about being a Jew in a nest of WASP privilege, does a good job of laying low: He moves his lips for The Lord's Prayer during chapel; he buries his Star of David necklace in a Band-Aid box; and he sneaks into the chapel postgame to observe Rosh Hashanah, although it means he has to recite his Hebrew prayers in front of a humongous cross.

David strives valiantly to deny himself and fit in, but thanks to a jealous school buddy (Matt Damon), everyone comes to learn that he's been living a lie. Now David faces losing his girl, his scholarship, and his college career because of the bigotry and hatred roiling in the hearts of those well-scrubbed prepsters. Moving his lips and burying his identity aren't going to work this time, and David's got to find a way to be true to himself and his ideals and yet fight the Goliath of a defense that's determined to hold the line and keep him from advancing.

Need a little courage boost in order to face that line of angry, self-righteous naysayers who want to knock you down and pressure you into denying who you truly are? Check out *School Ties* and see if it doesn't help you stand up for yourself and what you believe.

The truth shall set you free.

—John 8:32

Get Down Off the Cross, Someone Needs the Wood

*What I want to find in our marriage will remain my own concern.
I exact no promises and impose no obligations. Incidentally,
since it is of no importance to you, I love you.*
★ Raymond Massey as Gail Wynand in *The Fountainhead*

*Ordinarily, I don't like to be around interesting people because it
means I have to be interesting too.*
★ Steve Martin as Harris K. Telemacher in *L.A. Story*

*Oh, I'm such an old fool. These are only tears of gratitude—an old
maid's gratitude for the crumbs offered her.*
★ Bette Davis as Charlotte Vale in *Now, Voyager*
. . . continued

*Well, of course Aunt March prefers Amy over me. Why shouldn't
she? I'm ugly and awkward and I always say the wrong things.
I fly around throwing away perfectly good marriage proposals.
I love our home, but I'm just so dreadful and I can't stand
being here! I'm sorry, I'm sorry, Marmee. There's just
something really wrong with me. I want to change, but I—I
can't. And I just know I'll never fit in anywhere.*

★ Winona Ryder as Jo March in *Little Women*

▪ *The Sopranos Season 3* (2001)
Stars: Edie Falco, James Gandolfini, Lorraine Bracco
Created by: David Chase

We admit, a portrait of modern-day gangland set amid the marshlands of northern
New Jersey may seem like an unlikely place to go looking for tips on accepting personal
responsibility. The third season of *The Sopranos*, however, asks some very important questions about the limits of personal responsibility in marriage as this powerful husband and
wife play out a turf war between what they do and who they are, and how much each of
them is responsible for the other.

Carmela Soprano (Edie Falco) is the devoted and extremely Catholic wife of devoted
and extremely lapsed Catholic mob boss Tony Soprano (James Gandolfini). Tony and
Carmela live like most other upper-middle-class Upper Essex County professionals:
They have a stately home, an SUV, a built-in swimming pool, and trouble with their kids.
And they wrestle with the same issues we all do: rebellious teenagers, aging parents, a shift-
ing economy, and keeping the romance alive in a long-term relationship. The only difference is that Tony reports for work to a strip club at three in the morning, there are a lot of
people hanging around with names like Paulie Walnuts, and there's the occasional Fed with
a search warrant in his hand pounding on the front door.

These should be niggling details that are shoved under the rug for your typical Mafia wife. But Carmela is a new breed of Mafia wife—psychologically astute, socially and morally responsible, and less able to separate her husband from his misdeeds, or her own complicity from her own self-image. And yet this husband and wife really love each other, so the scale tips back and forth as they try to determine the extent of their own responsibility for the life of crime they lead, and the extent to which they are simply victims of their circumstances or each other.

This is a great series to watch when you're having trouble owning up to the obvious and figuring out who's to blame. *The Sopranos* reminds us that the only place we can really look for redemption is in the mirror, when at last we're ready to own up to our responsibilities and forge a better life.

Fuhgedaboudit

In Vegas, everybody's gotta watch everybody else. Since the players are looking to beat the casino, the dealers are watching the players. The box men are watching the dealers. The floor men are watching the box men. The pit bosses are watching the floor men. The shift bosses are watching the pit bosses. The casino manager is watching the shift bosses. I'm watching the casino manager. And the eye-in-the-sky is watching us all.
★ Robert De Niro as Ace Rothstein in *Casino*

I'm in the waste management business. Everybody immediately assumes you're mobbed up. It's a stereotype. And it's offensive.
★ James Gandolfini as Tony Soprano in *The Sopranos*

Just when I think I'm out, they pull me back in.
★ Al Pacino as Michael Corleone in *The Godfather*

Chapter 5

"Help! Jane! Stop This Crazy Thing!": Antianxiety Movies

Is your little engine that could running on high-anxiety octane? Is your emotional temperature gauge bleeding into the danger zone and you're worried about overheating on the highway of life? If you've got a case of the Level Orange blues, put down that panic button and pick up your remote control and your spirits with one of these Antianxiety Movies about worrywarts and overachievers just like you and me, who learn that the road to inner peace is paved with faith, self-reliance, a little creative distraction, and sometimes a damn good sense of humor.

▪ *The Ring* (2002)

Stars: *Naomi Watts, Martin Henderson, David Dorfman,*
    Brian Cox, Jane Alexander
Director: *Gore Verbinski*
Writers: *Ehren Kruger, Hiroshi Takahashi, based on the novel*
    Ringu *by Kôji Suzuki and the Japanese movie* Ringu

When you're in the midst of an anxiety attack, there's nothing like a good clean scare to make your terminal tension feel like a mild case of the butterflies by comparison. And *The Ring* may be one of the best over-the-counter desensitization prescriptions ever concocted, because this is one really scary movie.

Investigative reporter Rachel Keller (Naomi Watts) discovers a videotape that, once played, results in the viewer literally dying of fright within seven days. Since Rachel herself has seen the tape, as well as her ex-husband (Martin Henderson) and her son (David Dorfman), one can imagine that she's just a little bit anxious to get to the bottom of the sinister footage, whose fleeting and non-sequitur symbols look a lot like a Freudian nightmare committed to film . . . well . . . either that, or a trailer for a new Adrian Lyne movie.

Rachel's search for the root cause of these Memorex murders leads her to the wilds of the Pacific Northwest, where she literally must go to the very bottom of the well of dysfunction to uncover a legacy of abuse, and comfort the wounded inner child that still lingers there in the darkness.

Not only is this a masterfully constructed metaphor for the evils of subconscious compulsions and the very real value of psychotherapy, but this is also a truly creepy movie that will keep you on the edge of the couch and give those hypervigilant adrenal glands of yours a good workout, so you can get a restful night's sleep.

Here Comes Your Nineteenth Nervous Breakdown

The man's been through solid matter, for crying out loud! Who knows what's happened to his brain? Maybe it's scrambled his molecules! All I'm saying is, Mr. President, let's not panic!

★ William Traylor as General Catburd in *The Adventures of Buckaroo Banzai Across the 8th Dimension*

You fathers will understand. You have a little girl. She looks up to you. You're her oracle. You're her hero. And then the day comes when she gets her first permanent wave and goes to her first real party, and from that day on, you're in a constant state of panic.

★ Spencer Tracy as Stanley Banks in *Father of the Bride*

Upset? Upset is waking up and realizing somebody forgot to give you a belly button. Upset is realizing somebody took your nose to play Foosball. This ain't upset, kid. This is panic! I'm two squirts from being history!

★ John Goodman as Frosty in *Frosty Returns*

Wait a minute, fellows. I was just thinking. I really don't want to see the wizard this much. I'd better wait for you outside.

★ Bert Lahr as The Cowardly Lion in *The Wizard of Oz*

■ *Adaptation* (2002)
Stars: *Nicolas Cage, Meryl Streep, Chris Cooper*
Director: *Spike Jonze*
Writer: *Charlie Kaufman, based on the book* The Orchid Thief *by Susan Orlean*

Anxious about having to follow through on a promise you made in haste, but determined to honor your word? As this metascreenplay begins, screenwriter Charlie Kaufman (Nicolas Cage) is in just such a dilemma and, understandably, on the verge of full-fledged panic.

Seems Charlie, in a sudden burst of idealism and self-confidence, has taken on the task of adapting a quirky nonfiction book by a writer named Susan Orlean (Meryl Streep) into a full-length movie. But as his deadline clock ticks away, Charlie starts discovering that staying true to the essence of the source material—and the essence of good screenwriting—is causing him to throw buckets of cold water on any spark of an idea. Suddenly, his life is a series of false starts, sleepless nights, and explosions of manic but fruitless brainstorming. No wonder he has a powerful urge to murder his effervescent roommate, twin brother Donald (Nicolas Cage), who, unlike his anxiety-ridden brother, is cheerfully breezing through his own first screenplay. It's an absurd piece of commercial junk that follows all the rules and, much to Charlie's chagrin, will probably be a blockbuster hit on mall screens everywhere, while Charlie's creativity is yielding nothing more than excuses to his agent and Orlean.

So, like most of us who have faced that wall of dread and anxiety, the hapless Charlie has to learn to deconstruct his preconceived notions about himself and his work and find a new way to approach his task. Charlie has to swallow his pride, dig deeper, come at his problems from another angle . . . and stalk his inspiration, Orlean, in the hope that maybe she can help him out of this mess. It seems Charlie might make it out of his swamp of self-loathing and pessimism after all and come up with a wonderful screenplay.

This crazy romp is a great flick to watch when your mind is about to explode and you need a break from your own seemingly impossible challenge. Laughing at Charlie's obsessional spirals of self-doubt will free you up to believe once again that you really can fashion a miracle with the tools and materials you have.

∽

*It is good to tame the mind, which is difficult to hold in, and
flighty, rushing wherever it listeth.*

—Dhammapada

∽

▪ *Living in Oblivion* (1995)
Stars: Steve Buscemi, Catherine Keener, Dermot Mulroney, Danielle von Zerneck, James LeGros
Director and Writer: Tom DiCillo

They say that misery loves company, but so, apparently, does anxiety, because when you're wrapped too tight, there's nothing like watching some other poor schmuck get into a pickle and then panic to take a little of the torque off, and remind you not to sweat the small stuff.

In this director's nightmare, indie filmmaker (read: poor schmuck) Nick Reve (Steve Buscemi) spends the longest night of his life in a frantic attempt to capture the moment. Unfortunately, the moment keeps getting away from him as does the boom, the budget, Wolf the cameraman's left eye, leading man Chad Palomino's (James LeGros) ego, and the dwarf in the dream sequence's patience. Yet through all the incompetence, confusion, and emotional noise, Nick forges ahead in pursuit of his vision, armed only with his ability to maintain calm and keep his lens focused, which is hard when your cinematographer (Dermot Mulroney) is wearing an eye patch.

Finally, in the eleventh hour, with the light failing, booms dipping, frames unlocking, and dialogue falling flat, Nick resorts to the final refuge of poor schmucks everywhere . . . he freaks out. And then he slugs his leading man. Nick learns, however, as we all do eventually once the smoke from our spinning wheels clears, that there was no need to panic at all, because everything always works out in the end.

Watch this movie when you're feeling overwhelmed by the details of your current production. *Living in Oblivion* will not only have you laughing away your anxiety, but should remind you that while we may not end up with quite the same movie as we had originally envisioned up there on the screen, if we keep our cameras rolling, we will find our way to a happy ending.

Rave On

To begin . . . To begin . . . How to start? I'm
hungry. I should get coffee. Coffee would help me
think. Maybe I should write something first,
then reward myself with coffee. Coffee and a muffin. So I need to
establish the themes. Maybe a banana nut. That's a good muffin.

★ Nicolas Cage as Charlie Kaufman in *Adaptation*

Do I have an original thought in my head? My bald head. Maybe if I
were happier, my hair wouldn't be falling out. Life is short. I need to
make the most of it. Today is the first day of the rest of my life. I'm a
walking cliché. I really need to go to the doctor and have my leg
checked. There's something wrong. A bump. The dentist called again.
I'm way overdue. If I stop putting things off I would be happier.

★ Nicolas Cage as Charlie Kaufman in *Adaptation*

Have you ever had a dream with a dwarf in it? Do you know
anyone who's had a dream with a dwarf in it? No! I don't even
have dreams with dwarves in them. The only place I've seen
dwarves in dreams is in stupid movies like this! "Oh make it
weird, put a dwarf in it!" Everyone will go "Whoa, this must
be a fuckin' dream, there's a fuckin' dwarf in it!" Well I'm sick
of it! You can take this dream sequence and stick it up your ass!

★ Peter Dinklage as Tito the Dwarf in *Living in Oblivion*

Great! I freak out in your dream, I freak out in my dream, no
wonder I'm so fucking exhausted.

★ Steve Buscemi as Nick Reve in *Living in Oblivion*

▪ *To Kill a Mockingbird* (1962)

Stars: *Gregory Peck, Mary Badham, Phillip Alford, Brock Peters, Robert Duvall, Collin Wilcox Paxton, James Anderson, John Megna*
Director: *Robert Mulligan*
Writer: *Horton Foote, based on the novel by Harper Lee*

In little old Maycomb, Alabama, it's not just the children who are fearful of—and yet utterly fascinated by—anyone who is different. While little Scout (Mary Badham) and Jem Finch (Phillip Alford) and their friend Dill Harris (John Megna) innocently provoke the shadowy invalid Boo Radley into engaging with them, across town there's a lonely young woman who is needling a "colored" handyman to engage with her—sexually, that is. Needless to say, in a small Southern town during the Depression, the latter attempt at connecting with the object of one's fear and fascination has far more tragic consequences than the former. The tentative Boo (Robert Duvall) starts leaving little presents around for the kids to find. The handyman, Tom Robinson (Brock Peters), wisely tries to run away from a situation fraught with danger. Eventually, it all boils over into a kangaroo trial in which a white girl (Collin Wilcox Paxton) stammers out an accusation of rape against Tom. Egging her on is her redneck pappy (James Anderson) and his buddies, who are just itching to get this thang over with and start the hanging so they can continue in their ignorant, fearful, and backward ways.

And in the eye of this storm stands Atticus Finch (Gregory Peck), the kids' father and the handyman's lawyer, modeling calm reason, compassion, and understanding. It's a lesson that, sadly, falls on too many deaf ears in Maycomb. But somehow when we see little Scout guilelessly stand up to a lynch mob and say hello to her friend's pappy, or take the hand of Boo and flash him a trusting smile, we remember that even when adults are at their worst, there is always hope that we can rise above our darker nature and open ourselves to love and acceptance.

This is a great movie to watch when you are surrounded by a mob that's projecting its rage and fear outward and the voice of reason is just a whisper getting lost among the cacophony. Because even if it seems there's no Atticus Finch around to point out what is true and what is right, there's a little of him in all of us, if we can just have the courage to let him speak.

Reel to Real

Scout and Jem's little friend Dill Harris was based on author Harper Lee's real-life childhood friend Truman Capote. Capote wrote the book *In Cold Blood* about two outsiders who murder, and the novel *Breakfast at Tiffany's* about two outsiders who find love—and both were made into movies.

Things They Don't Sell at the Mall

Neighbors bring food with death, and flowers with sickness, and little things in between. Boo was our neighbor. He gave us two soap dolls, a broken watch and chain, a knife, and our lives.

★ Kim Stanley as the grown-up Scout Finch in *To Kill a Mockingbird*

■ *About Schmidt* (2002)
Stars: Jack Nicholson, Kathy Bates, Hope Davis, Dermot Mulroney
Director: Alexander Payne
Writers: Alexander Payne, Jim Taylor, based on the novel by Louis Begley

For years, retiring insurance salesman Warren Schmidt (Jack Nicholson) has avoided thinking about the smallness of his life, but his wife's sudden demise leads him to realize that if he dropped dead tomorrow his legacy would be a pile of office archives gathering dust in some storage facility, a house filled with ceramic thimble collections, and a distant daughter who is carrying on a tradition of numbing ordinariness.

Schmidt's need to matter to someone somewhere launches him on a panicky mission to convince his daughter, Jeannie (Hope Davis), to get on a path to a more glowing future. So he hops in an oversized RV and begins his crusade, headed to Denver to do his best to talk Jeannie out of marrying some water bed salesman in a mullet (Dermot Mulroney), whose greatest achievement in life was earning a handful of fading high school soccer ribbons bearing the words "for participation" and "honorable mention."

But once Schmidt finally gets a chance to stop smiling weakly at his soon-to-be in-laws, corner the harried Jeannie, and shatter her illusions about her fiancé, will she thank him profusely, seize the day, and go forth to live a life of adventure? Or will Schmidt have to find another way to quell his anxiety about having made no difference to anyone, and accept that his only child will marry a fellow whose dullness is a constant reminder of Schmidt's own undeniable mediocrity?

When you're starting to stress out over the meaning of your own life, *About Schmidt* is a gently funny reminder that in the end, the highway of fear and anxiety does not necessarily connect to the road to joy. So if you're looking for love and greater meaning, you'd better start by traveling inward and reaching out to the people who need you, and making connections. Then again, if you're planning to connect with them some night in a hot tub not too far from Boulder, you might want to clarify the bathing suit situation.

Bev's Culinarytherapy: Moisturizing Miracle for White Knuckles

If your hands are dry and cracked from clutching the steering wheel of life, try this moisturizing miracle for white knuckles, and for a few minutes, anyway, relax your grip on the controls.

Here's what you'll need:
¼ *cup sugar*
½ *cup olive oil*
1 *pair of surgical gloves with talc*

. . . *continued*

Here's how you do it:

Stir the sugar into the olive oil to make a thin paste. Coat your hands with the paste, then pull on the gloves and leave them on for 30 minutes. When you remove the gloves, your hands should be very soft.

■ *Far from Heaven* (2002)
Stars: Julianne Moore, Dennis Quaid, Dennis Haysbert
Director and Writer: Todd Haynes

There's nothing like an old-fashioned, sentimental, romantic movie about a golden-hearted but extremely naive woman whose life gets turned upside down to remind you that change doesn't have to paralyze you with fear.

Cathy Whitaker (Julianne Moore) is one of those Jane Wyman characters of classic tearjerker romances (in fact, this movie is eerily reminiscent of her 1955 movie with Rock Hudson, *All That Heaven Allows*—and for that matter it's also similar to 1992's *Love Field*, with Michelle Pfeiffer as the naive housewife and Dennis Haysbert as the kindly black man who befriends her). Cathy is the ideal late 1950s, upper-middle-class, jewel-toned-satin-and-petticoat-wearing suburban Connecticut housewife. The biggest problems in her life are making sure she hires just the right caterers for her latest community-service affair, keeping her son from using bad language like "geez" in her home, and matching her pumps to her pocketbook and elbow gloves. When Cathy's company-man husband, Frank (Dennis Quaid), starts getting busted outside of gay bars, she straightens her shoulders, throws her head back, and, like a good WASP, buries all her feelings about his homosexual tendencies. Yes, Cathy will unconditionally support her man in his quest to "beat this thing" via this newfangled psychotherapy stuff.

But when Cathy's perfect life begins to fall apart despite her Herculean efforts to keep things contained, she finally breaks down and confides in an eloquent and dignified "Negro" gardener (Dennis Haysbert once again in the Sidney Poitier role). This causes her family and friends to whip themselves into a frenzy of judgmental fury. Can Cathy find serenity and joy again? Will the pressures split apart the friendship that's holding her together? Will she finally blow this Popsicle stand and take up residence in a more cosmopolitan neck of the woods?

Watch *Far from Heaven* when you feel that no matter how well you're containing your fears, they're popping up like so many gophers in the garden. Because even when change seems bad, growth is always good.

Because of deep love, one is courageous.

—Lao-tzu

Nancy's Momentous Minutiae: The Waters of Compassion

Jimmy Stewart broke down sobbing while filming the tavern scene in *It's a Wonderful Life* in which George Bailey begins to pray.

In *The Wizard of Oz*, Judy Garland was supposed to sing "Over the Rainbow" a second time, when she's in the witch's castle and missing her home in Kansas. However, she and the crew all cried so much while filming the scene that the director decided to cut it out of the movie.

During the filming of *Splash*, vegetarian Daryl Hannah was served faux lobster inside shells for a dinner scene, yet still cried over the deaths of the poor creatures that'd inhabited the shells.

Words to Live By

For peace of mind, we need to resign as general manager of the universe.

★ science-fiction writer Larry Eisenberg

Nothing can bring you peace but yourself; nothing, but the triumph of principles.

★ Ralph Waldo Emerson

A peace that comes from fear and not from the heart is the opposite of peace.

★ Gersonides

■ *Panic Room* (2002)
Stars: Jodie Foster, Kristen Stewart, Forest Whitaker, Jared Leto, Dwight Yoakam
Director: David Fincher
Writer: David Koepp

We all have those anxious days when we wish that we could just close the door, lock the bolt, activate the alarm, and keep ourselves hermetically sealed off from danger. But as Meg Altman (Jodie Foster) and her daughter, Sarah (Kristen Stewart), learn, the only way to be truly safe is to find a way out of the panic room.

On the heels of a divorce, Meg Altman buys a brownstone for herself and her preteen daughter. One of the big lures of the house is "the panic room," a sanctuary guaranteed to be completely safe from intruders, disasters, and most acts of God. The idea of a hermetically sealed chamber, providing safety from the onslaught of life, is an attractive idea to a woman unexpectedly thrust out into the world without her male protector. And on their first night in their new home, Meg and Sarah get the chance to put the panic room through its paces when three burglars break and enter. What results is a feature-length siege between captive and captor that will not only exhaust your fight-or-flight responses and distract you from all of those circular obsessional thoughts, but remind you that the only way to be truly safe is not to close and lock your doors, but to open them and start reaching out for reinforcements.

Them's Fightin' Words

That's it then. Cancel the kitchen scraps for lepers and orphans, no more merciful beheadings, and call off Christmas!
★ Alan Rickman as the sheriff of Nottingham
in *Robin Hood: Prince of Thieves*

I will live with you in this hellhole, but I must express myself. If you don't let me gut out this house and make it my own, I will go insane and I will take you with me!
★ Catherine O'Hara as Delia in *Beetlejuice*

This pretentious, ponderous collection of religious rock psalms is enough to prompt the question "What day did the Lord create Spiñal Tap, and couldn't he have rested on that day too?"
★ Rob Reiner as Marty DeBergi reading from
an album review in *This Is Spiñal Tap*

Don't point that finger at me unless you intend to use it.
★ Walter Matthau as Oscar Madison in *The Odd Couple*

. . . continued

We deal in lead, my friend.

★ Steve McQueen as Vin in *The Magnificent Seven*

Don't mess with the volcano, my man, 'cause I will go Pompeii on your butt.

★ Ben Stiller as Mr. Furious in *Mystery Men*

Murray, lend me twenty dollars or I'll call your wife and tell her you're in Central Park wearing a dress.

★ Walter Matthau as Oscar Madison in *The Odd Couple*

I warn you, scoundrel, I was trained at the King's Academy and schooled in weaponry by the palace guard. You stand no chance. When you run, I shall ride, when you stop, the steel of this strap shall be lodged in your brain.

★ Hugh Jackman as Leopold in *Kate & Leopold*

That would be perpetuating the fantasy! It's not dealing with the problem. I have a therapist to answer to!

★ Marisa Tomei as Ruby Weaver in *Happy Accidents*

■ *Defending Your Life* (1991)
Stars: Albert Brooks, Meryl Streep, Rip Torn, Lee Grant, Buck Henry, Shirley MacLaine
Director and Writer: Albert Brooks

Fear feeds upon fear, and as this quirky little comedy about one man's experience with purgatory shows, you have to let go of your insecurities and take a risk now and again in order to grow spiritually. Oh, and in purgatory, everybody's unfailingly polite and accommodating, and the food's great, so we can only imagine how delightful heaven must be.

Unlike most of the oldsters walking around Judgment City, that great midwestern metropolis of the dead somewhere in the sky, Dan Miller (Albert Brooks) left the land of the living in middle age when he plowed his brand-new BMW into a bus in a moment of stupid distraction. Apparently, stupid distractions are something one has to answer for in the afterlife, as Dan learns when he gets to Judgment City. Just like all the other recent dead, he has to leave behind the all-you-can-eat-with-no-calories-or-cholesterol buffets at a comfy hotel and board a tram downtown, to go on trial for his life.

There are plenty of activities to keep one's mind off that fatal day of reckoning, like three championship golf courses, comedy clubs, and the Past Lives Pavilion, where you can meet your past lives (the hostess is, of course, a hologram of Shirley MacLaine). And you do get free legal representation. And yes, if one of the highlights of your life was rescuing your adopted children and their fluffy cat from a fire, like his new friend Julia (Meryl Streep) did, the whole trial thing is probably just a formality. But if you're a nervous, fear-driven person trying desperately to outmaneuver the wisdom of the universe, you're going to have to switch gears and open yourself up to a less frantic way of existing.

If the thought of taking a fearless self-inventory sets off a panic attack, take a deep breath, watch *Defending Your Life*, and reassure yourself that you really can free yourself from some of that crippling anxiety.

 ## Words to Live By

Fear is like a giant fog. It sits on your brain
and blocks everything—real feelings, true
happiness, real joy. They can't get through that fog. But you lift it
and buddy, you're in for the ride of your life.
★ Rip Torn as Bob Diamond in *Defending Your Life*

Don't Burn Your Hair in Satan's Lair

Despite our best efforts to make it through those pearly gates, we mustn't forget that good intentions can lead straight to hell. So what's in store for those of us who end up on the wrong side of the earthly divide, in a world of eternal punishment? Well, according to Hollywood, things might not be so bad after all. Here's a road map to the underworld and its princes of darkness that you might want to tuck away in a back pocket, just in case. Oh, and if you're headed to the land of eternal punishment, you may want to don jewel-tone crushed velvet, as Satan apparently is rather fond of the look.

Bill and Ted's Bogus Journey (1991)

Satan is an oversized horned red demon with fierce teeth, and hell is a place where boot camp sergeants demand an infinite number of push-ups (no girlie ones either!), and you relive your foolish childhood traumas involving kissing mustached grandmas. But you are allowed to leave if you challenge the Grim Reaper and beat him. (Hint: Forget about Battleship and Clue—Twister's the game that'll win your freedom, 'cause Death may be scary but he sure isn't limber.)

Deconstructing Harry (1997)

Hell is most conveniently reached by the service elevator, and of course there's a special floor for serial killers and lawyers who appear on TV (just above the floor for the media). Amid the smell of burning sulfur and orange lighting, and the sight of lots of naked people writhing in half-agony, half-ecstasy, you will find Satan himself. Satan looks a lot like Billy Crystal in a black crushed-velvet jacket and spandex turtleneck, doing his Fernando

. . . continued

lounge lizard act, only without the accent. The good news is that while it's awful hot down there, Satan does offer martinis and top-shelf tequila, and even air-conditioning (after all, AC counts as evil when you consider its effect on the ozone, Satan politely points out).

Angel Heart (1987)

Satan is a distinguished gentleman named Louis Cyphre who bears an uncanny resemblance to Robert De Niro, in a well-kempt beard and pulled-back black hair, wearing a black suit, and tapping his long, creepy, immaculately manicured, and pointy fingernails on his walking stick. Satan is quite polite, even appreciative of a fine cup of cappuccino in one of those cute little cafés in Little Italy. However, he's a businessman who insists on having his clients honor their contracts, so don't sign anything without reading the fine print. And hell? That would be the psychological torment of being an amnesiac serial killer whose crimes are worthy of an NC-17 rating—and that's not even the director's cut.

Bedazzled (1967)

Satan, played by screenwriter Stanley Donan, looks just like the *Help!*-era George Harrison in tiny wire-rim glasses and a black cape, and sporting a British accent. When he's not helping his clients to use up their seven wishes (which they get in exchange for their soul), he's running an underground club, expiring parking meters prematurely, and destroying WET PAINT signs. Evil as he may seem, he's really just misunderstood and waiting for his chance to take that service elevator up to God's greenhouse in the sky and plead his case for reinstatement in heaven. Hey, we understand taking the service elevator to hell, but shouldn't there be a nice polished oak number if you're on your way up to paradise?

. . . continued

Bedazzled (2000)

Yes, it's true: Satan is a supermodel. She has offices in hell, purgatory, and L.A., and she drives a black Lamborghini Diablo. And being the Elizabeth Hurley–supermodel type, she flouts her stuff in one body-clinging, male-fantasy outfit after another, from black leather jeans and a mini T-shirt with "Bad" written on it in pink rhinestones to the requisite cut-down-to-there red spaghetti-strap minidress. Satan's actually a friendly sort, making helpful little suggestions to her latest conquest (played by Brendan Fraser) about how best to use the seven wishes he gets in exchange for his soul. But cross her, and she will revert to that traditional horned, yellow-eyed, trident-bearing beast surrounded by fireballs.

Little Nicky (2000)

Satan is almost sexy in a Harvey Keitel kind of way, with his stylish goatee, understated horns, and crushed velvet suit. Satan's pop, Lucifer, gave up his throne ten thousand years ago and walks around in his robe being ineffectual and getting no respect (of course, he's played by Rodney Dangerfield). As for hell, well, yes, it's pretty hot, but there's a certain justice there—Hitler's eternal punishment is appropriately scatological—and Satan's son Little Nicky's corner of it is pretty radical, dude, with Metallica posters, an electric guitar that is always plugged in, and Ozzy Osbourne classics on the stereo. Just watch your step with all that steam shooting up from the floor and the lightning flashes.

End of Days (1999)

Satan, an evil force created by one of those computerized-effects generators to look like a rippling heat wave, whooshes like a jet engine into the men's room in a nice Italian restaurant and possesses the body of Gabriel Byrne.

. . . continued

So in human form, Satan is a devilishly handsome black Irishman in an impeccable black suit and overcoat with upturned collar. He's got a wicked sense of humor, a lustful twinkle in his eye, the ability to set off fireballs wherever he goes, and of course, evil of all evils, he smokes. Under stress, however, he does revert to one of those humongous winged gargoyles surrounded by fire, and as one might guess happens in an Arnold Schwarzenegger action movie, Satan blows things up real good.

Devil's Advocate (1997)
Satan is a lawyer. Need we say more?

▪ *Waiting for Guffman* (1996)
Stars: *Christopher Guest, Eugene Levy, Parker Posey, Catherine O'Hara,*
Fred Willard
Director: *Christopher Guest*
Writers: *Christopher Guest, Eugene Levy*

There's nothing like a story about a bunch of really bad community theater actors to make you feel a little less anxious about your own performance. And Christopher "*Spinal Tap*" Guest's hilarious portrait of community theater celebrity presents one of the most god-awful plays within a play ever committed to film.

When the good citizens of Blaine, Missouri, decide to put on a play to celebrate their sesquicentennial, they gather together the best talent that Main Street U.S.A. has to offer. Which isn't saying a lot. There's Corky St. Clair (Christopher Guest), a failed musical theater actor with dreams of becoming a great director; Ron and Sheila (Fred Willard and Catherine O'Hara), a husband-and-wife travel agent team that has never been out of town; Libby Mae Brown (Parker Posey), a girl in the trailer next door who dreams of going to the Big Apple and watching TV with Italian guys; and Allen Pearl (Eugene Levy), a dentist who dreams of being a stand-up comedian.

Needless to say, when this motley crew of misguided players gets together to hold their fun house mirror up to life, the absurd reflection shining back at us not only provides us with a healthy dose of comic relief, but reminds us that we are all just poor players upon a community theater stage, so ham it up! Because in the end, the only true failures are the people who don't enjoy the show.

Ignorance Is Bliss

We are the luckiest sons of bitches in the world,
  you know that?
  ★ Leonardo DiCaprio as Jack Dawson in *Titanic*

He's teaching me to change my instincts . . . or at least ignore
  them.
  ★ Catherine O'Hara as Sheila Albertson in *Waiting for Guffman*

There'll always be a place for me at the DQ.
  ★ Parker Posey as Libby Mae Brown in *Waiting for Guffman*

And I promise you I'll never desert you again because after **Salome**
  we'll make another picture and another picture. You see, this is
  my life! It always will be! Nothing else! Just us, the cameras,
  and those wonderful people out there in the dark! All right,
  Mr. DeMille, I'm ready for my close-up.
  ★ Gloria Swanson as Norma Desmond in *Sunset Boulevard*

Give Peace a Chance

It's easy to love thy enemies when they're lovable. But if your enemy acts—well, like an enemy—it's only natural to feel that lofty pronouncements such as "turn the other cheek" and "give him your cloak as well" call for some modifications.

When you're ready to blow your top at someone you disagree with, let off a little steam with these movies that speak to the heart about finding nonviolent solutions.

The Quiet American (2002)
Stars: Michael Caine, Brendan Fraser, Do Thi Hai Yen
Director: Phillip Noyce
Writers: Christopher Hampton, Robert Schenkkan, based on the novel
  by Graham Greene

Love is supposed to lift us up, but sometimes our assumptions about how love ought to be result in bullying behavior that's just not worthy of us.

Alden Pyle (Brendan Fraser) is just a "quiet American" with a ready smile, a closet full of crisp-even-in-the-rainy-season suits, a can-do eagerness to help the Vietnamese people, and lots of dubious explanations for his associations with shady businessmen and politicians. Pyle falls madly in love with a gorgeous young Vietnamese woman, Phuong (Do Thi Hai Yen). Problem is, Phuong is already mistress to a middle-aged British journalist named Thomas Fowler, played by Michael Caine, whose big, gentle brown eyes and tender glances allow him to pull off a pairing that normally would make us groan about Hollywood trying to make old geezer actors look sexy by giving them love scenes with twentysomethings.

Anyway, while Phuong can't marry a Vietnamese man because she's not a virgin and Fowler's wife won't give him a divorce, Phuong is content for now

. . . continued

with the love Fowler offers. She may not have a lot of choices in life, but, hey, this is the one she picks. Pyle, however, is certain that Phuong can't possibly be happy unless she's married with children in a nice nuclear American-style family unit headed by a benign patriarch—namely, him. Of course, this is all one big metaphor for American hegemony that stomps on the heads of people who really aren't asking to be saved, or fixed, or whisked away to a better life.

Watch *The Quiet American* when you're at an impasse with someone—maybe it will help you have a greater appreciation for the grace and beauty of compromise.

Love is patient, love is kind. Love is not envious, or boastful, or arrogant, or rude. It does not insist on its own way. It is not irritable, or resentful. It does not rejoice in wrongdoing but rejoices in the truth.

—Cor. 13:4–6

Changing Lanes (2002)
Stars: Ben Affleck, Samuel L. Jackson, Sydney Pollack
Director: Roger Michell
Writers: Chap Taylor, Michael Tolkin, based on a story by Chap Taylor

In all our rushing about we can find ourselves getting caught up in fear, frustration, and self-absorption. Our frenzy builds from windstorm to all-destructive tornado that destroys just about everything in its path until finally we're left alone to contemplate whether it wouldn't have been easier to just take a deep breath and say "I'm sorry."

Ah, but Gavin Banek (Ben Affleck) is a busy, busy lawyer. Why, he's late for his date to cheat some lovely young woman out of control of her late

. . . *continued*

grandfather's charitable trust! In his rush, he plows into Doyle Gipson's (Samuel L. Jackson) car on a busy expressway. Does he stop to chat, learn that Doyle is headed to the courthouse as well for a child custody hearing, and offer him a lift to make up for smashing his car? Heck no. The narcissistic Gavin dashes off, not realizing he's just left an excruciatingly important court document in the hands of one very pissed-off man who is just itching for a scapegoat for his considerable life problems. Thus ensues a cat-and-mouse game that completely occupies both men all day, blinding them to practical and ethical options that would solve both of their problems, and costing them far more than they would ever have dreamed of gambling. Nope, they couldn't just take five seconds and do a little Ujai breathing.

Feeling rushed and pressured? Take a couple of hours to enjoy this engaging cautionary tale about two men who learn the hard way that not allowing time for reflection, or for simple niceties toward other people, can put you in the fast lane toward personal disaster. So take a break and feel proud of yourself for leaving some breathing space between you and chaos.

Where wisdom is called for, force is of little use.
—Herodotus

Gimme Shelter (1970)
Stars: Mick Jagger, Keith Richards, Mick Taylor, Charlie Watts, Bill Wyman
Directors: David Maysles, Albert Maysles, Charlotte Zwerin

It was 1970 and the echoes of Woodstock were reverberating across the land. While the violence of the Vietnam War continued thousands of miles away, a half a million kids had been able to spend an entire weekend in the mud and rain

. . . continued

in some cow field in Upstate New York and experience peace, harmony, rock and roll, and major psychedelic drugs. So hey, why not try it again on the West Coast?

Unfortunately, as we see in this concert documentary, peace is not something to be taken for granted. At the Altamont Speedway in San Francisco, where the Rolling Stones were playing a free show for charity, three hundred thousand kids weren't exactly getting back to the garden. Maybe it was the cold that accounted for the angry, distrustful vibe. Maybe it was the jinx of the Stones playing the song "Sympathy for the Devil," which even Mick Jagger admitted always seemed to lead to something "funny" happening—although that doesn't quite explain why some Hell's Angel went onstage and bashed in the face of the Jefferson Airplane's guitarist earlier in the afternoon. No, it was probably due to the security provided by none other than the Hell's Angels, who are the last people that should come to mind when one thinks of peace, love, and harmony. Hired to sit on the edge of the stage, drink all the free beer they wanted, and keep all the cats in line, the bikers didn't exactly rise to the occasion. And even those flower children passing out roses and holding up huge yarn God's eyes, and Mick Jagger in Renaissance velvet knickers and ruffled shirt with a hand on his hip, pleading, "Brothers and sisters, come on now, that means everybody, just cool out," weren't enough to bring out everyone's inner Buddhist.

Hey, we're all for releasing primal instincts on occasion, particularly when they involve groovin' to blues-based classic rock. But as this movie shows, peace requires effort, and sometimes we're all in need of some restraint. And if you don't want violence, it's probably not a good idea to mix every known mood-altering substance with a crowd of three hundred thousand, and hire really big, beer-buzzed Hell's Angels wielding sticks and knives to keep them at bay.

It is the discretion of a man to be slow to anger, and it is his glory to pass over a transgression.

—Prov. 19:11

■ *An American Rhapsody* (2001)
Stars: Scarlett Johansson, Nastassja Kinski, Tony Goldwyn, Larisa Oleynik
Director and Writer: Éva Gárdos

Sometimes the truth about the past is so painful that it seems the best course is to lock it up in a little box and bury it in a closet somewhere. But as this powerful coming-of-age movie shows, if we want to achieve intimacy we have to stop being afraid of pain and rejection and be willing to embrace our bad memories, share them with the one we love, and talk about the taboo subjects. At least, this is the lesson Margit Sandor (Nastassja Kinski) has to learn, but it takes her daughter blowing a shotgun through her ranch house bedroom door to get through to her.

Suzanne (Scarlett Johansson) is a typical early sixties California teenage girl, with ponytail, pedal pushers, and pouty look every time her mother asks her where she's going. For all the distractions of boys and booze, however, Suzanne still can't keep her mind off what's really eating at her—not knowing where she belongs or why her mother left her, but not her sister, behind the Iron Curtain when she was an infant. Suzanne had been raised by a wonderful couple with a farm, only to be whisked away to America six years later with no explanations. How could her mother have abandoned her without so much as an "I'm sorry" when they met again? Suzanne doesn't know where her home is, who her "real" mother is, or what her center is. She is desperate to take a journey of self-discovery, but her mother's more inclined to call the locksmith and have him install bars on Suzanne's bedroom windows and doors.

When you're in the mood for a healing message about letting go and loving more fully, watch *An American Rhapsody* and free yourself from the prison of fear.

The difficult problems in life always start off being simple.

—Tao Te Ching

▪ *Dog Day Afternoon* (1975)
Stars: Al Pacino, Penny Allen, John Cazale, James Broderick
Director: Sidney Lumet
Writer: Frank Pierson, based on an article by P. F. Kluge and Thomas Moore

If you feel like you're living in a Murphy's Law world, and things just keep going from bad to worse, spend a couple of hours with the unluckiest man in Brooklyn, and make yourself feel a little better about yourself by comparison.

Out of work, and unable to support his wife and children, or fund a sex-change operation for his boyfriend, Sonny (Al Pacino) gets the brilliant idea of robbing a bank. Unfortunately, aside from having absolutely no talent for crime whatsoever, Sonny also has a series of bad breaks that turn a ten-minute bank heist into a ten-hour standoff with the NYPD, the FBI, and a SWAT team, not to mention a coast-to-coast media blitz that catapults him into a dubious infamy. And the best part is, the whole story is true.

So if you've been developing a little bit of a Job complex, and you're feeling like a rock-and-a-hard-place sandwich, let poor Sonny's doomed yet eccentrically heroic battle against his own bottom line remind you that the first trick in beating anxiety is to avoid getting in over your head, and that the price of refusing to accept what you can't change is a lifetime spent raging against the machine.

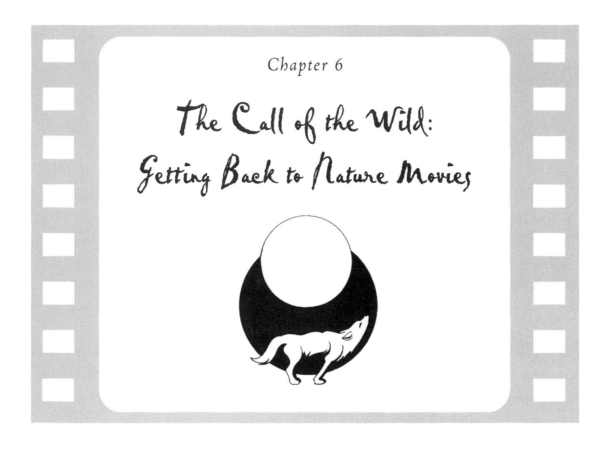

Chapter 6

The Call of the Wild: Getting Back to Nature Movies

Are you suffocating in an asphalt jungle? Feeling alienated, dissociated, and soulless? If you're longing to get back in touch with the soul of the universe and reconnect with nature but you can't manage a trip to the wild side this weekend, go on a walkabout with one of these Getting Back to Nature Movies featuring wanderers, wayfarers, and pioneers who forge new paths into the wilderness and learn the lessons that the natural world has to teach us. You'll get back to the core of your own nature without ever having to leave your living room.

∎ *Keep the River on Your Right* (2000)

Star: Tobias Schneebaum
Directors: David Shapiro, Laurie Shapiro

This documentary follows gay anthropologist Tobias Schneebaum as he retraces the trail he blazed through the Amazon Basin nearly forty-five years earlier—a trail marked only with the words "Keep the river on your right."

For Tobias, a seventy-eight-year-old man with Parkinson's disease, there are a lot of formidable enemies hiding in the jungle. There's the rain and the mud that coats everything with a thin layer of silt, making river crossings treacherous for an elderly wanderer, for whom a broken hip could mean never walking again. And then there's the coincidental meeting with his former native lover and friend, Aipit, with whom Tobias is joyfully reunited only to have to leave him once more, this time probably forever.

And finally there is the Tarakambut tribe itself, which years ago led Tobias into the wild heart of the jungle that simultaneously set him free and ensnared him. But despite the howls in the night, Tobias pushes forward, through the mud and the memories, back to the bosom of the family that adopted him all those years ago, with whom he identified so profoundly that he even participated in their sexual ceremonies, ate human flesh, and was transformed from an urbane, hypercivilized New York painter on holiday into a modern cannibal who would never paint again.

Along Tobias's trail through the Amazon Basin, we get a sometimes startling but always enlightening view of some of the most fundamental contradictions in nature: birth and death, age and youth, love and loss, humanity and brutality. Through Tobias Schneebaum's eyes we come to understand that even in the darkest part of the jungle there is light, that in letting go we bring love closer, that in poverty there is wealth, in aging, youth, and in the grip of death, an embrace.

■ *Frontier House* (2002)
 Stars: *Gordon Clune, Adrienne Clune, Mark Glenn, Karen Glenn,*
  Nate Brooks, Kristen Brooks
 Director: *Maro Chermayeff*

This six-hour PBS documentary about three families re-creating frontier life in the American West is like *Survivor* gone highbrow. It makes you appreciate that getting back to nature also means getting back to human nature, which, as *Frontier House* reveals, can get damn ugly when you've been doing manual labor all day while dressed head-to-toe in nineteenth-century woolen garb.

The Glenn family from Tennessee is lucky enough to draw the straw that lets them have a fully completed house for the duration of a summer spent as pioneers in Montana. The Clunes—four kids and two parents from a ritzy section of L.A.—have to start out with only the foundation for their dwelling, while Nate Brooks and his elderly dad from back east are given a book on how to build your log cabin and a few weeks to raise the walls so that Nate's fiancée can join the project. At first the families are all cordial to each other and certain that they are of the sturdy stock that could survive a winter on the frontier after only a few months' preparations. But soon their animals begin to get sick or wander off, a freak snowstorm hits, hands get painfully raw, the boredom of monotony sets in, bellies groan for more calories, and hair gets authentically matted down with gunk (this is, after all, the pre-shampoo era). Suddenly, the *Little House on the Prairie* optimism starts giving way to Hatfields-and-McCoys rivalries. Somebody starts bending, then breaking, the rules of the project and claiming that hey, cheating's the American way. Somebody else starts finding that the only real amusement at the end of a long day in the middle of nowhere is to bitch about those folks down the road. And somebody's marriage is souring faster than fresh milk in the blistering August sun.

Thinking you want to chuck it all and start over with a tent under the stars and a can-do attitude? Indulge in this engaging and eye-opening series and see if it doesn't sober you up to the reality that roughing it doesn't always put one in the mood for spiritual communion with one's fellow man.

You Can't Fool Mother Nature

If you're longing to be reminded that there
is something larger than you are, or just need to
be reassured that no matter how bad the storm,
there is always a morning after, seek shelter with one
of these You Can't Fool Mother Nature Movies, and
be inspired to hold out until the rescue boat arrives with
the dawn.

Deep Impact (1998)
Stars: Robert Duvall, Téa Leoni, Elijah Wood, Vanessa Redgrave,
    Morgan Freeman
Director: Mimi Leder
Writers: Bruce Joel Rubin, Michael Tolkin

When an asteroid the size of California threatens to slam into earth,
President Beck (Morgan Freeman), Jenny (Téa Leoni), a fledgling reporter
with a nose for news, and Leo (Elijah Wood), a teenage astronomer with a
superhero streak, join forces to try and avert the impact of an ELE (which
stands for Extinction Level Event and is pronounced like "Ellie"). Leave it to
Hollywood to name the end of the world after a woman.

    Will man triumph over meteor, or will life on Earth come to an end?
When you're in the mood to confront the force of fusion physics, watch *Deep
Impact* and see if you can outrun gravity.

. . . continued

Titanic (1997)
Stars: Leonardo DiCaprio, Kate Winslet, Kathy Bates, Frances Fisher
Director and Writer: James Cameron

The story of history's sunken monument to man's arrogance is well known to us all. What does come as a surprise, though, is that in this version of the mighty *Titanic's* mythic fall from grace, they've cast Leonardo DiCaprio in what is clearly a Jack Nicholson role, and still managed to stay afloat at the box office. Well, we guess that the attraction of young girls to cherubic and golden-haired male waifs who are emblematic of the doomed beauty of youth is another one of the immutable forces of nature that we can all rely upon.

Twister (1996)
Stars: Helen Hunt, Bill Paxton, Cary Elwes, Jami Gertz,
  Philip Seymour Hoffman
Director: Jan de Bont
Writers: Michael Crichton, Anne-Marie Martin

Is this tornado a metaphor for a stormy divorce, or is the stormy divorce a metaphor for the catastrophic force of a tornado? Watch Jo (Helen Hunt) and Bill (Bill Paxton) try to rekindle their flame in the eye of a tornado, and you be the judge. . . .But one thing is for sure: This movie will remind you that when you go chasing after the wind, you reap the whirlwind!

. . . *continued*

Sunny Side Up

Cities fall but they are rebuilt. Heroes
die but they are remembered.

    ★ Morgan Freeman as President Beck in *Deep Impact*

Mr. President, I'm not saying we wouldn't get our hair
mussed. But I do say no more than ten to twenty
million killed, tops. Uh, depending on the breaks.

    ★ George C. Scott as Gen. "Buck" Turgidson
in *Dr. Strangelove*

That's the one good thing about Paris: There's a lot
of girls willing to take their clothes off.

    ★ Leonardo DiCaprio as Jack in *Titanic*

I love waking up in the morning not knowing where
I'm gonna go or who I'm gonna meet. Just the
other night I was sleeping under a bridge, and
now here I am, on the grandest ship in the
world, having champagne with you fine people.

    ★ Leonardo DiCaprio as Jack in *Titanic*

When you used to tell me that you chase tornadoes,
deep down I thought it was just a metaphor.

    ★ Jami Gertz as Melissa in *Twister*

■ *Cast Away* (2000)
Stars: *Tom Hanks, Helen Hunt, Chris Noth*
Director: *Robert Zemeckis*
Writer: *William Broyles Jr.*

If the chatter of your big-city life is making it hard for you to hear your soul speak, then spend a few hours with the castaway in his bungalow built for one and get back in touch with the fundamentals.

Tom Hanks stars as an overachieving FedEx exec who lives and dies by the clock. Neither rain nor sleet nor Iron Curtains nor marriage proposals nor even Christmas dinner can keep this new-millennium postman from making his appointed rounds. Nothing, that is, until his plane crashes over the ocean and he washes up on a deserted island, and remains marooned there for nearly a decade with only the sun, the sand, the surf, and a volleyball named Wilson who never talks back for company. In fact, there is so little dialogue, mostly just waves talking to the tide, that this movie can function like a sort of wave machine with pictures.

So if you're feeling deaf to the quiet voice inside that reminds you of what's really important, get back to the cradle of evolution with *Cast Away*, and reconnect.

■ *Mary Shelley's Frankenstein* (1994)
Stars: *Kenneth Branagh, Robert De Niro, Helena Bonham Carter,*
    Tom Hulce, Aidan Quinn, Ian Holm, John Cleese
Director: *Kenneth Branagh*
Writers: *Steph Lady, Frank Darabont, based on the novel by Mary Shelley*

Nature can be cruel and seemingly fickle, but as this movie—far more true to the novel than all those Boris Karloff versions—shows, nature has its own wisdom that exceeds our ability to replicate it without a lot of rough seams and grotesquely inferior reproductions.

Dolly the Sheep and genetic engineering are centuries away, but Victor Frankenstein (Kenneth Branagh) is a scientific zealot who is even wackier than those Raelians. In an era when cholera plagues and death in childbirth are commonplace, Frankenstein is determined to reverse nature's course. He ignores the warnings of his friend (Tom Hulce) and mentor (John Cleese) about trying to fool Mother Nature and cobbles together a creature (Robert De Niro) from a piece of this and a piece of that, then vivifies him. Only instead of doing the responsible thing and finding a place for this patchwork creature in the grand web of life, Frankenstein basically freaks out, abandons his "baby," and hightails it out of town.

So where shall this creature find contentment and companionship? What happens when a being with human emotions is denied the right to love? Why are people so quick to judge and reject? And does everyone in eighteenth-century England have a stash of gasoline-soaked torches around so they can form an angry, frightened posse on a moment's notice?

Beyond the lightning flashes, moments of terror and violence, and gruesome special effects, this is a movie that will provoke more than an adrenaline rush. It'll have you pondering the awesome wisdom of nature and its intricate web.

Junk Food for the Soul

Swept Away (2002)
Stars: Madonna, Adriano Giannini, Bruce Greenwood
Director: Guy Ritchie
Writers: Lina Wertmüller, Guy Ritchie

Leave it to Madonna and Guy Ritchie to shoot straight for the heart of the primordial battle of the sexes and come out of that Freudian wilderness with nothing to show for it but a rape fantasy that plays like an *I Dream of Jeannie* episode set on *Gilligan's Island*.

. . . continued

Madonna stars as Amber (read: Ginger), a spoiled jet-setter, bored and disgusted with even the finest that life has to offer, who suddenly fixates all of her existential ennui on Pepe (Adriano Giannini), the unwashed and somewhat slightly dazed but still extremely sexy Europroletariat/cabin boy. While on a yacht sailing to some rich-blooded playground or another with her magnate husband, Tony (Bruce Greenwood), Amber takes every opportunity to emasculate Pepe, whom she calls Pee Pee. Which, we have to admit, does sum up his character pretty adequately. But when Amber winds up marooned with this Euro-Gilligan on an uncharted desert isle and must rely on him to provide the essentials of survival, Ginger instantly transforms into Jeannie, Euro-Gilligan into a naïf *sauvage* version of Major Nelson, and Jeannie starts calling the Pee Pee "Master." Definitely less Lina Wertmüller and more Sherwood Schwartz.

Now, it's very easy to take shots at this movie because it's so unabashedly bad. But what makes *Swept Away* Junk Food for the Soul is the film's idea that if we go back to the garden, and we remove all of the evil capitalist ideals and restrictive social conventions that cast us out in the first place, then Eve will realize that she sort of likes getting slapped around, and that maybe Adam's serpent isn't so bad after all, and paradise on earth will come again. Our idea of paradise is a garden where we have weeded out movies like this one that suggest that female dominance lies in a woman's power to enjoy and exploit her own submission. I mean, I guess "If you can't beat them join them" is a workable philosophy, but wouldn't it be better just to dispense with the sir/slave sexual politics of the disco era altogether?

Words to Live By

*Look at the world today. Is there anything
more pitiful? What madness there is!
What blindness! What unintelligent leadership! A scurrying
mass of bewildered humanity crashing headlong against each
other, compelled by an orgy of greed and brutality. The time
must come, my friend, when this orgy will spend itself, when
brutality and the lust for power must perish by its own sword.*
★ Sam Jaffe as the High Lama in *Lost Horizon*

You do not find peace by avoiding life, Leonard.
★ Nicole Kidman as Virginia Woolf in *The Hours*

■ **The Secret of Roan Inish** (1994)

*Stars: Jeni Courtney, Mick Lally, Eileen Colgan, Richard Sheridan,
Dave Duffy*

Director: John Sayles

Writer: John Sayles, based on the novel The Secret of the Ron Mor Skerry *by
Rosalie K. Fry*

When you're feeling disconnected from nature and tired of measuring time by clocks instead of tides, this magical and exquisite little movie is a tonic for the soul.

Because her widowed and grieving father (Dave Duffy) is spending far too many hours bending an elbow at the pub and she is becoming pale and frail in the city, little Fiona Coneely (Jeni Courtney) is sent to live with her grandparents (Mick Lally and Eileen

Colgan) on the west coast of Ireland. It's a land of rolling verdant hills and fields of purple and yellow wildflowers, dotted with white cottages that Martha Stewart would call distressed but the locals would call in need of a limestone paint job and some new thatching. Grandma and Grandpa are salt-of-the-earth folks who still manage to eke out a living from the sea and the land, but are increasingly feeling the pressure to admit defeat, leave it all behind, and depart the countryside for some loud, polluted city as the younger folks have.

Fiona, however, becomes entranced by their folktales of selkies—seals that transform into women. She becomes convinced that the sea, which so cruelly snatched away her infant brother a few years back, can be coaxed into returning him. So Fiona and her cousin Eamon (Richard Sheridan) begin to believe that when you love the land, respect the power of the sea, and are willing to engage in a lot of hard manual labor, magic happens. But is Fiona a child with way too much time on her hands, mesmerized by too many fishermen's tales about lost little boys sailing around in wooden cradle ships? Or will the sea and the seals be able to return to the Coneelys that which was torn from their souls, and once again make them feel whole and connected to those they love?

When you're feeling beleaguered, make time for timelessness, watch *The Secret of Roan Inish*, and be inspired to commune with the water, the wind, and the land.

You will find something more in woods than in books.
Trees and stones will teach you that which you can never learn
from masters.

—St. Bernard

The Jack Factor: No Matter Where You Go, There You Are

While a walk in the woods may do wonders to cleanse the soul, it's no substitute for psychotherapy or a reliable antidepressant. As these disgruntled wayfarers, all played by Jack Nicholson, show, when it comes to the wilderness of a dark obsession, no matter where you go, there you are.

The Shining (1980)
Stars: Jack Nicholson, Shelley Duvall, Scatman Crothers, Danny Lloyd
Director: Stanley Kubrick
Writer: Stanley Kubrick, based on the novel by Stephen King

Not even holing up in an abandoned hotel in the Rocky Mountains in the dead of winter can keep trouble from Jack's door in this dysfunctional thriller that pits the nuclear American family against the darkest impulses of human nature. Jack (Jack Nicholson) and Wendy Torrance (Shelley Duvall) accept a job in Estes Park as caretakers of a hotel that is only open in the summer because the roads are impassable all winter. They hope that once there, amid the solace of the snow, elk, and aspen trees, Jack will find the quiet place inside himself, stop being quite so angry at his family, and start on that book he's been meaning to write. Unfortunately, not even the towering Indian peaks can overshadow the treacherous highs and lows of Jack's altitudinous dysfunction, and it isn't too long before the rage comes home to roost.

. . . continued

The Pledge (2001)
Stars: Jack Nicholson, Patricia Clarkson
Director: Sean Penn
Writer: Jerzy Kromolowski, based on the novel by Friedrich Dürrenmatt

There's nothing like a police thriller to remind us all that when it comes to obsession and compulsion, you can run, but you can't hide. On the eve of his retirement party, Jerry Black (Jack Nicholson) responds to a call about a murdered little girl, and that night pledges to the grieving mother (Patricia Clarkson) that he will bring the killer to justice. And when they arrest a man Jerry believes is innocent, he heads into the high-country desert in search of the truth and some freedom from the compulsions that have haunted his working life. Unfortunately, this poor character is being played by Jack Nicholson, who is emblematic of the uncontrollable impulses of nature within us all, and so the roadside cafés and trout streams of Nevada only serve to fuel his insatiable inner appetites, and no matter where he goes, there he is.

■ **Born Free** (1966)
Stars: Virginia McKenna, Bill Travers, Geoffrey Keen—and Girl, Boy, Ugas, Henrietta, Mara, and the cubs
Directors: James Hill, Tom McGowan
Writer: Lester Cole, based on the book by Joy Adamson

Born Free is a classic lesson in how we must respect nature enough to suppress our human instinct to protect a wild animal from the harsh landscape of, well, the wild.

Joy Adamson (Virginia McKenna) is the wife of George Adamson (Bill Travers), a British game warden working in Africa, and one day she is delighted to discover that her husband has brought home three orphaned lion cubs. All of Joy's maternal instinct buttons are pushed and she stays up late into the night adjusting her recipe for baby lion milk in order to find a formula that they will drink. But it's the runt of the litter, Elsa, who truly captures Joy's heart. She's bright and curious, but she's so small and weak that she probably wouldn't survive on the savannah. Luckily, Elsa has Joy to be her friend and surrogate mother. And when the time comes for Elsa to return to the wild, Joy is determined to fight the odds and help her learn the survival skills that will allow her to live free, just as she was born free.

Now, Joy has an endlessly supportive husband (who sure gets a lot of time off from his day job) and complete devotion to fostering her beloved Elsa's independence, but if she continues to feed Elsa instead of forcing her to learn to hunt or starve, Elsa will end up dead or in a zoo. And yet, if she succeeds in retraining Elsa, will Joy ever again nuzzle her furry face and hear her thunderous purring?

If you've been struggling with wanting to protect and hold on to someone you love, watch *Born Free* and be reminded that nature has its own wisdom, harsh as it may seem at times, and that letting go doesn't have to mean saying good-bye forever.

'Tis a Gift to Be Simple

*I wear my sort of clothes to save me the trouble of
deciding which clothes to wear.*
★ Katharine Hepburn

I base most of my fashion taste on what doesn't itch.
★ Gilda Radner

■ *Greystoke:* The Legend of Tarzan, Lord of the Apes (1984)
Stars: Christopher Lambert, Ian Holm, Ralph Richardson, Andie MacDowell
Director: Hugh Hudson
Writers: Robert Towne, Michael Austin, based on the novel Tarzan of the Apes
by Edgar Rice Burroughs

Unlike most of those Tarzan movies featuring a stocky guy in a silly cheetah-skin loin-cloth yodeling his way across the jungle one vine at a time, *Greystoke* tells the story of a man who has to come to terms with his own nature—and human nature—in order to know where his home is.

John (Christopher Lambert) is just a baby when he and his parents are shipwrecked somewhere in the rain forests of Africa. Malaria takes his mother's life and a gorilla takes his father's, leaving little Lord Greystoke, heir to an estate back in merry old England, to be raised by an ape. The boy doesn't realize he's human, as he's never seen a "white ape" until Phillippe (Ian Holm), a Belgian victim of an ambush, shows up and explains that there's a whole other world waiting for him. And more important from John's point of view, back in London he has a grandfather (Ralph Richardson) deeply longing for a reunion.

Under the Belgian's tutelage, John quickly defies Noam Chomsky's theories of language acquisition and human development and, lickety split, masters the queen's English as well as French. And then there are a few other tricks he has to pick up over the next several months in order to take his proper place in British society—not slurping his soup, tying an ascot, walking upright, etc. But for John, of course, it's all worth it to be once again in the arms of family. Then the brutality and inhumanity inherent in the underbelly of upper-class Victorian society has to go and rear its ugly head. Now who is the man, who is the beast, and where does John truly belong? Can he deny his animal nature? Can he turn his back on his heritage and the woman he loves (Andie MacDowell)? Can he stop with the brooding glances and gorilla hooting in the bedroom? 'Cause they're really just waaaay too sexy.

Anyway, with all that we've learned about anthropology and human development since the Tarzan books were written, this movie may seem just too preposterous. But if you're in the mood for a provocative exploration into the nature of who we really are, check out *Greystoke.*

Too Much Monkey Business

What better way to explore one's primal nature than through imagining an upside-down society where apes are civilized and humans are wild beasts? In one of the most successful science-fiction series of all time—the Planet of the Apes franchise—all the big questions are raised: What gives man his divine spark? What sets us apart from beasts? How do apes that can't figure out how to make a paper airplane manage to fix a time-traveling spaceship, or launch a nuclear holocaust? What are those chimps always sniffing at? And how can we milk this concept for every potential merchandising dollar?

Here's our map to the planet of the apes and its unique time line and worldview.

Planet of the Apes (1968)

It all starts when three astronauts with three different motives for space exploration crash-land on a planet, thousands of years after leaving Earth. Back home, the big questions facing humankind were how man could be so brutal as to invent war and terrorism, hatred and racism, and why we could put a man in space but not find a way to love each other despite our differences? On the planet of the apes, however, the question becomes, how the hell do we get out of here, and why did we leave home in the first place?

Hulking gorillas treat mute human herds like prey. Orangutans pompously lecture on the ape version of creationism while overseeing experimental brain surgery on people. And a couple of gentle chimpanzees with degrees in the soft sciences are the only hope that the last surviving human, the

. . . continued

misanthropic Taylor (Charlton Heston), can stay alive and get back to the human society for which he now has a greater appreciation.

Together, Zira (Kim Hunter), Cornelius (Roddy McDowall), and Taylor set off for the secrets of The Forbidden Zone. What they learn is fodder for deep reflection—and a slew of sequels of varying quality.

Beneath the Planet of the Apes (1970)

James Franciscus comes forward in time to rescue Taylor, who is being held by a cult of telepathic mutants living underground. Despite the efforts of the hippie apes who just want to give peace a chance, nuclear holocaust ensues, destroying all life, but not the potential for more sequels.

Escape from the Planet of the Apes (1971)

Just as their planet is being destroyed by nuclear holocaust, clever chimps Cornelius and Zira find and fix Taylor's spaceship and time-travel back to the seventies. They try to get along with all races, creeds, and levels of primate, but our heroes fall to the destructive force of human fear of the unknown— of course, not before setting us up for . . .

Conquest of the Planet of the Apes (1972)

Yes, Zira managed to give birth to Caesar (Roddy McDowall), just in the nick of time before succumbing to human violence. Caesar has been carefully hidden by a circus trainer (Ricardo Montalban) because humans, familiar with the plot sequence by now, fear that someday talking apes will take over Earth. Like his fellow apes, Caesar is a slave relegated to washing windows and acting subservient instead of living up to his potential to, er, rule the planet. He bravely starts an ape revolution that gives birth to a new society where a creature is not judged on the hairiness of his skin but by the content of his character. That is, until . . .

. . . continued

Battle for the Planet of the Apes (1973)

Oh, you know that peace couldn't last with all those warmongering humans and boneheaded gorillas about. This sequel's an excuse for one big battle scene, culminating in a network TV series, lunch boxes, Halloween costumes, action figure sets, and of course, yet one more movie . . .

Planet of the Apes (2001)

Mark Wahlberg is a scientist who just can't bear to sacrifice his favorite chimp in the name of science and recklessly follows the little guy through a porthole to a planet where apes rule men. He meets up with a Zira-esque chimp with an open mind (Helena Bonham Carter) who, though she's not much on extended conversations that shed light on the nature of man versus the nature of animal, does manage to get Marky Mark and his pals out of this upside-down world. And now the only question that remains is, can we all get along without yet another illogical and provocative kitsch sequel to this series?

■ *Lost Horizon* (1937)

Stars: Ronald Colman, John Howard, Sam Jaffe, Jane Wyatt
Director: Frank Capra
Writer: Robert Riskin, based on the novel by James Hilton

This classic utopian story will inspire you to believe that you *can* chuck it all and get back to your authentic, ageless self.

Having just helped a band of Europeans and Americans escape civil war in China while leaving the natives behind to face their grim fate, British diplomat Robert "Bob" Conway (Ronald Colman) is in a whiskey-swilling, what's-it-all-about? kind of mood. So he's up for an adventure when he discovers that he and his four fellow airplane passengers have been kidnapped by the pilot and are traveling deep into uncharted territory in the Himalayas.

A plane wreck ensues, and the survivors are rescued and taken to Shangri-La, which is an extraordinary mountain village somewhere in Tibet, a place untouched by time, money, crime, war, or the Chinese government's "concern" for the natives. In Shangri-La, you can take a breather and just enjoy good food, good service, and philosophizing on the nature of man. Well, that is, as long as you're of European ancestry. For the natives, it seems, meaning is found in postcard-pretty work like making candles and shearing sheep. (Hey, it's a 1937 film, ya gotta make some allowances.)

Anyway, as Bob learns more about the mysteries of the place, he and the others develop vacation head and aren't anxious to go back to their old lives. But can they really say no to their responsibilities back home? Can Bob convince his brother (John Howard) to embrace utopia? Can the women find a motivation for staying or going that has nothing to do with some guy they've fallen in love with?

When you're tired of modern-day pressures, *Lost Horizon* will remind you that yes, snowcapped mountains, waterfalls that drop into warm little ponds, and cherry trees in bloom can get anyone back in touch with his or her spiritual nature. It's just that sometimes the journey to your Shangri-La can be arduous and the map hard to read.

Viewers' Note: The original film negative deteriorated so badly that some scenes have been replaced by stills with soundtrack accompaniment.

A journey of a thousand miles starts with one step.

—Tao Te Ching

■ *Seven Years in Tibet* (1997)
Stars: Brad Pitt, B. D. Wong, Jamyang Jamtsho Wangchuk
Director: Jean-Jacques Annaud
Writer: Becky Johnston, based on the book by Heinrich Harrer

Brad Pitt stars as Heinrich Harrer, an Austrian Nazi sympathizer who leaves Austria to climb a mountain on the verge of world war. When he's halfway up the Himalayas, war breaks out, and Heinrich and his reluctant companion must climb to the nearest town, which turns out to be none other than the holy city and the home of the Dalai Lama (Jamyang Jamtsho Wangchuk). Heinrich and the Dalai Lama hit it off immediately, and together they begin to build a collective utopia in the heart of the Himalayan highlands that looks a lot like a Tibetan version of Neverland.

In the seven years it takes to get Heinrich through the Himalayas, eyes are opened, hearts are touched, adults are led to the truth by children, empires fall, empires rise, and Heinrich turns out to be a pretty nice guy after all, which we always knew, because of the adorable way that one golden curl dances angelically in the winds of the Tibetan summer.

If you're just hungry for a little scenery and don't want to think about much beyond the next bend in the mountain trail or the next flutter of Brad Pitt's transcendental locks as he hikes up over the next Himalayan peak, than pop in this feature-length Tibetan screen saver of a movie, crank up the AC, light the incense, and say ommmmmmm.

Words to Live By

We have a saying in Tibet: If a problem can be solved, there is no use worrying about it. If it can't be solved, worrying will do no good.

★ Jamyang Jamtsho Wangchuk as the Dalai Lama
in *Seven Years in Tibet*

▪ *Arachnophobia* (1990)
Stars: *Jeff Daniels, Harley Jane Kozak, John Goodman*
Director: *Frank Marshall*
Writers: *Don Jakoby, Wesley Strick, based on a story by Don Jakoby and*
  Al Williams

Nobody can walk on the wild side like an arachnid, and when a cluster of large and really lethal spiders are accidentally transported from the rain forest into a sleepy California bedroom community, we all get a taste of what life is like in the jungle.

When young, handsome, and city-weary Doc Jennings (Jeff Daniels) moves his young family to a small California town far away from the crime and grime of L.A., he's looking forward to a return to a simpler and more innocent lifestyle, where the days are long and the nights are safe. But the country doesn't turn out to be quite what the doctor ordered, when small-town U.S.A. becomes infested with deadly spiders from some remote and highly contagious rain forest or another and Doc Jennings's new patients start dropping like flies. In the end Doc Jennings must join forces with his wife (Harley Jane Kozak) and the town exterminator, Delbert (John Goodman), and, most important, face his own arachnophobia, to save his family, pack his car, and drive back to the concrete jungle, which at this point seems infinitely safer than the real one.

The clearest way into the universe is through a forest wilderness.
—John Muir

■ *Never Cry Wolf* (1983)
Stars: Charles Martin Smith, Brian Dennehy, Zachary Ittimangnaq, Samson Jorah
Director: Carroll Ballard
Writers: Sam Hamm, Richard Kletter, Ralph Furmaniak, narration written by
    Charles Martin Smith, Eugene Corr, Christina Luescher, based on the book
    by Farley Mowat

The caribou are disappearing and Tyler (Charles Martin Smith) has a government grant to fly to the arctic circle, set up camp, and figure out if the wolves are to blame. Sheer dumb luck allows Tyler to survive the flight in a barely airborne private plane piloted by the cowboyish Rosie (Brian Dennehy). And despite having to make some hard decisions about what the essentials are—a crate of toilet paper or a crate of Moose beer?—Tyler is thrilled to be living out his childhood fantasy of going off into the wilderness. He's certain he'll reconnect with his visceral self and his survival instincts and become a new, stronger, braver man. Well, he definitely becomes a man with altered bathroom habits and a high tolerance for rodent infestations. And you really don't want to know what he ends up eating when the food rations get low.

Yes, Tyler becomes one with nature, but he also learns that even this far into the wilderness, civilization has a way of encroaching and mucking everything up. What will he do when the spring comes and he's committed to wrapping up Project Lupine and returning to civilization?

This is one of those sweeping vistas, how-the-heck-did-they-ever-get-a-camera-crew-in-there movies that will get you thinking about your own compromises with nature, and with your own nature. Watch it when you're feeling like your authentic self needs room to roam and see if it doesn't inspire you to forget—for just a little while—about clocks, projects, and limitations on your freedom.

Chapter 7

You Can Change the World: Power of One Movies

Are you mad as hell and you don't want to take it anymore, but you're feeling powerless to fight city hall? If you're ready to make a difference, but you're wondering what one person can do, start small with one of the Power of One Movies. These films are about local heroes and heroines who think globally and act locally, and through sheer determination, compassion, courage, and conviction, manage to move mountains, just by asking the right questions.

■ *Bowling for Columbine* (2002)

Stars: Michael Moore, Charlton Heston, Marilyn Manson, Dick Clark
Director and Writer: Michael Moore

Michael Moore isn't a wizened sage spouting aphorisms and poetic truths—he's a regular Joe with a camera, a mike, some hard questions, and a handy-dandy map to the stars' homes. In this documentary, which is at turns outrageously funny and deeply sobering, he doesn't find a lot of answers. But this movie shows that asking questions is a big part of "the" answer.

Why, asks Moore, do Americans shoot each other so often? Why do some outcasts turn to violence and suicide while others are able to rise above and transform their pain into laughter? What does bowling have to do with Columbine? And how can we Americans stop pumping bullets into each other?

Hmm . . . for starters, Moore suggests that we might consider making it a little more difficult to buy ammo than asking some pimply kid in a polyester smock at Kmart to slip a key into a cheap lock and start pulling out boxes of bullets for anyone who asks. Another way might be to stop whipping ourselves into mass hysteria about everything from violence in the street (despite irrefutable evidence that it's on the wane) to killer African bees. Another might be to remember that we're all Americans, and yes, we actually can look out for each other and not have to be prepared for imminent attack from the fella next door. And hey, what's up with those Canadians, who have plenty of guns and yet enough confidence in their neighbors to leave their doors unlocked?

This is a movie that proves that when we feel paralyzed by our inability to change the world, progress begins with the courage to ask hard questions and be willing to listen to the answers, regardless of how uncomfortable they make us.

Inquiring Minds Want to Know

Well, here's my first question. Do you think it's kind of dangerous handing out guns at a bank?
★ Michael Moore to a bank manager in *Bowling for Columbine*

The Constitution says you've got the right to bear arms. What do you think "arms" means? . . .What about nuclear weapons? Should you be able to have weapons-grade plutonium?
★ Michael Moore to John Nichols, brother of Oklahoma City bombing conspirator Terry Nichols, in *Bowling for Columbine*

Michael Moore: If you were to talk directly to the kids at Columbine or the people in that community, what would you say to them if they were here right now?
Marilyn Manson: I wouldn't say a single word to them. I would listen to what they have to say, and that's what no one did.
★ from *Bowling for Columbine*

■ *All the President's Men* (1976)
Stars: Robert Redford, Dustin Hoffman, Jason Robards, Hal Holbrook, Jane Alexander
Director: Alan J. Pakula
Writer: William Goldman, based on the book by Carl Bernstein and Bob Woodward

Based on a true story, this movie chronicles the real-life investigation by reporters that ultimately led to Nixon's resignation, which just goes to show you, when you ask the right questions, you can even fight the White House.

On the cusp of the 1972 elections, *Washington Post* reporter Bob Woodward (Robert Redford) is assigned to cover a break-in at the Democratic National Headquarters in the

Watergate Hotel. What begins as a routine investigation into a run-of-the-mill robbery, however, turns into a David-and-Goliath-style battle against the Washington power elite waged by two regular beat reporters, who are armed only with the sword of truth. Together, Woodward and Carl Bernstein (Dustin Hoffman) uncover a scandal that extends all the way to the giant in the oval office. As they follow the paper trail back to its origin and close in on the truth, Woodward and Bernstein face threats, intimidation, suspicion, and fear. Their nose for news, and their ultimate faith in the value of the truth, sustains them, however, and in the end, the scandal is revealed, the tapes are subpoenaed, and President Nixon resigns.

If you've got a bone to pick with the powers that be, but you're not sure what you can do about it because you can't fight city hall, let alone the White House, let Woodward and Bernstein inspire you to say it loud and say it proud. They'll reassure you that you can make a difference, just by insisting on the truth. Because even in Washington, the pen is mightier than the slush fund.

There is nothing better than to know that you don't know.

—Tao Te Ching

■ *The Wild Child* (1969)
Stars: Jean-Pierre Cargol, Françoise Seigner, François Truffaut
Director: François Truffaut
Writers: Jean Gruault, François Truffaut, based on the book Mémoires et rapport
  sur Victor de l'Aveyron *by Jean Itard*

On a summer day in 1798, in the woods of France, local farmers discover a feral child who seems more animal than human. A teacher at an institute for deaf children takes it upon himself to bring out the intelligence of this seemingly deaf-mute boy and even kindle the flames of his noble human nature. But first on his to-do list: Get the kid away from the flocks of tourists who swarm by the institute to gawk as if they were looking at a circus freak.

In this classic film, based on a true story, Dr. Jean Itard (François Truffaut) takes the newly discovered wild child (Jean-Pierre Cargol) to his humble French home in the countryside, where sunlight streams in and the doors are always open to the gentle breezes of summer, and the housekeeper, Madame Guerin (Françoise Seigner), always has an understanding smile and a glass of cool water to offer. Itard and Guerin provide the boy, now named Victor, with a stable environment, a predictable routine, and opportunities to frolic in the fields. Victor is disciplined with a progressive attitude for the time, and given a simple but challenging schedule of tasks designed to teach him the rudiments of living among people, and basic communication (although learning to speak may well be beyond his abilities).

Thanks to his instinctive grasp of child development and his appreciation for what motivates Victor, Itard makes formidable progress. But can he get the boy to understand the higher, abstract ideals that make us human? Will Victor ever fully feel that he is at home with the human race?

This movie's a wonderful lesson in not writing off the seemingly unteachable, and a testament to the power we have to affect the lives of others when we are willing to accept them as they are before we try to improve or fix them.

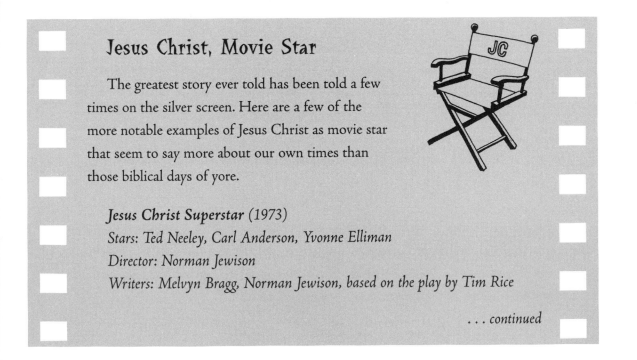

Jesus Christ, Movie Star

The greatest story ever told has been told a few times on the silver screen. Here are a few of the more notable examples of Jesus Christ as movie star that seem to say more about our own times than those biblical days of yore.

Jesus Christ Superstar (1973)
Stars: Ted Neeley, Carl Anderson, Yvonne Elliman
Director: Norman Jewison
Writers: Melvyn Bragg, Norman Jewison, based on the play by Tim Rice

. . . continued

This version of the passion play casts JC (Ted Neeley) as a sixties-style love child in long hair and sandals who belts out his gospel like a rock anthem, hangs around with beggars and prostitutes in his downtime, takes on the oppression inherent in the system, and ultimately ascends to rock god heaven after an early and tragic death at the hands of a corrupt establishment. Watch this one when you need to feel that God is not only on your side, but is probably a very viable choice as headliner at your next rock relief global simulcast.

Godspell (1973)
Stars: Victor Garber, David Haskell
Director: David Greene
Writers: David Greene, John-Michael Tebelak

A seventies camp classic, *Godspell* presents a warm and fuzzy—and decidedly nonthreatening and asexual—Jesus who wears rainbow suspenders, a Superman T-shirt, painted tears, and a white-boy-afro wig. The updated JC (Victor Garber) is paternalistic and moody as he tells parables in King Jamesian English to a bright-eyed group of hippies who dance and face-paint their way to enlightenment while belting out rock ballads like "When Wilt Thou Save the People" in a manner frighteningly reminiscent of those stagy kids on *Barney and Friends* or one of those embarrassing acting exercises designed to free performers from inhibitions that they should probably hold on to.

Watch this when you're in the mood for a kinder, gentler Judeo-Christian patriarch who shows mercy to those who practice bad theater improv and reminds us all that if you want to get to heaven, all you have to do is embrace your inner clown. Honk Honk.

. . . *continued*

The Last Temptation of Christ (1988)
Stars: Willem Dafoe, Harvey Keitel, Barbara Hershey
Director: Martin Scorsese
Writer: Paul Schrader, based on the novel by Nikos Kazantzakis

This is the urban, gritty, eighties-style interpretation of the passion play as only Scorsese can tell it, with lots of atmospheric slow-mo dolly shots, the clipped bare-bones dialogue of the street, a moody soundtrack, a Judas from Delancey Street (Harvey Keitel), and a fiercely human Jesus Christ (Willem Dafoe) who must overcome a guilty conscience and moral confusion to complete his mission here on Earth. Watch this when you need to remember that even our most celebrated archetypal heroes have to wrestle with the dark side.

Jesus of Montreal (1989)
Stars: Lothaire Bluteau, Catherine Wilkening
Director and Writer: Denys Arcand

Christianity and the Stanislavsky system meet in this Canadian film about a group of actors who are hired by their local parish to update and perform the passion play. When the actors begin internalizing their roles, and reinterpreting the Gospel with a radical bent, their method performances begin to rattle the powers that be as they head toward a crucifixion of a whole different color. Watch this when you need to remember that sometimes being Christlike means not being afraid to wreck the temple.

■ *Austin Powers in Goldmember* (2002)
Stars: *Mike Myers, Beyoncé Knowles, Seth Green, Michael York,*
    Robert Wagner, Mindy Sterling, Michael Caine, Verne Troyer
Director: *Jay Roach*
Writer: *Mike Myers*

In this supersized, superhero world of ours, we can all get to feeling a little small and insignificant by comparison. But as *Goldmember* reminds us, superheroes are only people like you and me who find a way to make a difference, just by being themselves.

Our favorite British hero with an atrocious overbite time-travels to his own past to rescue his father and save the world. And as if that weren't Freudian enough, he returns to the year 1975, and his own adolescence, where he must help his nemesis, Dr. Evil, confront his fractured father issues in order to save the world from his destructive patriarchal rage, years down the line.

This movie is a lovingly constructed time capsule from a bygone era when flowers had power, when feelin' groovy was a life goal, and when we really believed that we could change the world, just by changing ourselves.

Eternal Questions

Are those frickin' sharks with frickin' laser
beams attached to their frickin' heads?
 ★   Mike Myers as Dr. Evil in *Austin Powers in Goldmember*

I'm from Holland! Isn't that vierd?
 ★   Mike Myers as Goldmember in *Austin Powers in Goldmember*

Are you a clone of an angel?
 ★   Verne Troyer as Mini Me in *Austin Powers in Goldmember*

Junk Food for the Soul

***Kindergarten Cop* (1990)**
Stars: *Arnold Schwarzenegger, Linda Hunt,*
    Penelope Ann Miller, Pamela Reed,
    Joseph Cousins, Christian Cousins
Director: *Ivan Reitman*
Writers: *Murray Salem, Herschel Weingrod, Timothy Harris,*
    based on a story by Murray Salem

With *kindergarten* in the title and a passel of cute kids whose adorable antics drive tough guy Schwarzenegger bonkers, you might mistake this for a family friendly movie about a cop who learns nonviolent ways to solve problems because—shhhh! the children are watching! But no. Instead, this flick vacillates between cutesy-poo and disturbingly bloody.

When we first meet Detective John Kimble (Arnold Schwarzenegger), he has no qualms about drawing a gun or opening fire in a crowded beauty salon or party full of innocent bystanders. Hey, he'll get those evil felons even if he has to risk lives and inflict post-traumatic stress disorder onto dozens of frightened people. Then Kimble finds himself having to pinch-hit for a sick colleague (Pamela Reed) and go undercover as a kindergarten teacher in a small-town elementary school to smoke out a frightened mother (Penelope Ann Miller) and child (Joseph Cousins and Christian Cousins) who don't realize that a drug dealer is after them.

Kimble gets tough with the implausibly hyperdestructive "brats" in his class and shows them the value of military discipline and jumping jacks

. . . continued

(apparently there is no physical education in the school until a man comes along), and smiles indulgently at the jelly-kneed and desperate-for-a-man mothers in the community. What's more, he reassures the ladies that even though there aren't many daddies around, no one need worry about those little boys. If they play with dolls, Arnie will make sure that they only use them to act out looking up girls' dresses. Hardee har har.

Ultimately, Kimble's willingness to resort to violence to solve every problem is celebrated by all as some sort of glorious male warrior instinct instead of a mule-headed insistence on simplistic solutions for complex problems. Even the school principal (Linda Hunt) gazes at his muscles adoringly. Well, what can you expect of an administrator who, when some strange man shows up claiming to be FBI, immediately escorts him to the nearest group of vulnerable children?

This is a movie about how silly and weak women and children are, and how they can't be trusted with the truth, and instead need a big ol' cowboy with a semiautomatic weapon looking out for them—and about how a good daddy is a gun-happy daddy. When a movie can make a goofball like Jon Lovitz in a satire like *High School High* (see review p. 132) look like a model teacher by comparison, you've gotta wonder.

▪ *Blackboard Jungle* (1955)

Stars: Glenn Ford, Anne Francis, Sidney Poitier, Vic Morrow
Director: Richard Brooks
Writer: Richard Brooks, based on the novel by Evan Hunter

In this classic teacher-as-crusader movie, as Bill Haley urges everyone to get primal and rock around the clock, a first-year teacher named Richard Dadier (Glenn Ford) has to deal with the cynicism of his colleagues, the juvenile delinquent behavior of his students, and his own doubts if he's to survive, triumph, and make a difference. And he has to do it all without that set of six-guns Glenn Ford always has in all his Westerns. He even has to face down a switchblade in the hands of one student, Artie West (Vic Morrow), who's headed straight to reform school with that perpetual "wanna-make-me" mug.

Even though Dadier's youthful wife (Anne Francis) is terrorized by anonymous notes, and Dadier suffers a beating at the hands of West's gang, he's convinced that if he can just win over Miller (Sidney Poitier), the smart but wary kid who has leadership potential, the kids will come into line and he will actually have a chance to educate the boys at the bottom rung of a failing New York City public school.

For all its quaint period details—like a couple of pompadoured boys jitterbugging in the school yard and a gleeful teacher using a reel-to-reel tape recorder to get his students interested in "high-tech" learning—the story here feels far more contemporary than you might think. So if it seems that you're fighting the good fight all alone, watch *Blackboard Jungle* and be reassured that you can inspire others to join you.

Golden Apples All Around

Tough guys don't do math. Tough guys fry chicken for a living!

★ Edward James Olmos as Jaime Escalante in *Stand and Deliver*

Discipline is not the enemy of enthusiasm.

★ Morgan Freeman as Joe Clark in *Lean on Me*

Yeah, I've been beaten up, but I'm not beaten. I'm not beaten, and I'm not quittin'.

★ Glenn Ford as Richard Dadier in *Blackboard Jungle*

Miss Jean Brodie (Maggie Smith): To me, "education" is a leading out. The word "education" comes from the root "ex" meaning "out" and "duco," "I lead." To me, education is simply a leading out of what is already there.

Principal Emily Mackay (Celia Johnson): I had hoped that there might also be a certain amount of putting in . . .

Miss Jean Brodie: That would not be "education" but "intrusion," from the root prefix "en" meaning "in" and the stem "trudo" or "thrust," ergo, to thrust a lot of information into a pupil's head.

★ from *The Prime of Miss Jean Brodie*

Obedience without understanding is a blindness too.

★ Anne Bancroft as Annie Sullivan in *The Miracle Worker*

. . . continued

If you must play these petty games, then do them in your homes . . . and not in my classroom!
★ Sidney Poitier as Mark Thackeray in *To Sir, with Love*

Playing music is supposed to be fun. It's about heart, it's about feelings, moving people, and something beautiful, and it's not about notes on a page. I can teach you notes on a page, I can't teach you that other stuff.
★ Richard Dreyfuss as Glenn Holland in *Mr. Holland's Opus*

Well, I guess you can cut the arts as much as you want, Gene. Sooner or later, these kids aren't going to have anything to read or write about.
★ Richard Dreyfuss as Glenn Holland in *Mr. Holland's Opus*

■ *High School High* (1996)
Stars: Jon Lovitz, Tia Carrere, Louise Fletcher, Mekhi Phifer
Director: Hart Bochner
Writers: David Zucker, Robert LoCash, Pat Proft

We love how this movie manages to reinforce all of *Blackboard Jungle's* messages about believing in young people and the power of one teacher against an uncaring administration, while spoofing it at the same time. This is one of those laugh-out-loud funny flicks where even the minor sight gags are ingenious (our favorite: the student's "fade" haircut that serves as a track for two Matchbox cars zooming around his head).

History teacher Richard Clark (Jon Lovitz) is tired of living in the shadow of his father, who runs a snooty prep school, so he resigns to take a position at an inner city school to see if he can cut it on his own, without Dad's help.

Richard is so idealistic he misses all the obvious signs that he's up against a tough crowd. Clue number one: The school's name is Marion Barry High. Clue number two: The school's vending machine sells cans of malt liquor. Clue number three: The principal (Louise Fletcher) swings blunt instruments at students passing by her in the hallways. No, Richard's convinced that these kids are just like any others, eager to learn if someone will just believe in them.

Defying the odds, Clark teams up with an admiring administrative assistant, Miss Chapell (Tia Carrere), and wins the trust of his pupils—okay, so he does it by accident when he bails out of a car during a game of chicken that he somehow got caught up in. But when forces conspire to cheat the students out of their newfound confidence, and his top student (Mekhi Phifer) starts to give up on himself, Clark has to go that extra mile to bring everyone back into the fold. This results in an absurd plot twist that somehow finds Jon Lovitz wearing a tea ball from one ear and talkin' street as he infiltrates the local crank-dealers' lair.

When you're sorely in need of a few hours of laughing while being reassured that one man really can transform an urban war zone filled with junior thugs into a well-manicured haven for bright-eyed pupils in coordinating pastels, check out *High School High*.

■ *The Prime of Miss Jean Brodie* (1969)
Star: Maggie Smith
Director: Ronald Neame
Writer: Jay Presson Allen, based on his play and the novel by Muriel Spark

A teacher in a Scottish girls' boarding school in the 1930s, Miss Jean Brodie (Maggie Smith) has definite ideas about everything from free love to the Italian masters to how far one may open a window before committing the sin of vulgarity. As she explains to her young charges each semester, she is in her pr-r-r-rime, dedicated to her girls, and uninterested in the maintenance of the status quo, which just leads to petrification. And for all her stiff backbone, Miss Brodie is hardly petrified. In fact, she's an outspoken free spirit who savors sensuality, whether in the form of pâté de fois gras at an afternoon picnic, rich purple frocks that capture her joie de vivre, or passionate love affairs with men to whom she is not married.

Now, the board of directors allows Miss Brodie to indulge in her passions when they result in girls who gleefully tour museums on the weekend and aspire to goodness, truth, and beauty just like their mentor does. However, they're not so keen on free love, so Miss Brodie does her best to maintain discretion in that department. But she's not willing to become a spinster in a brown dress and a bun, and the expectations of how she ought to act become so stifling that ultimately she begins to use poor judgment about how to release the pressure.

Alas, Miss Brodie learns the hard way that when one is unwilling to compromise one's enthusiasm and idealism and conform ever so slightly to the rules of the establishment—despite how silly or bourgeois they may seem—one makes enemies of those who envy the nonconformist spirit. And worse, one also ends up handing said enemies exactly the ammunition they need to take you down. After all, ebullience is one thing, but encouraging youthful sexual exploration and impetuous trips to the front to fight for idealistic fascist dictators are different matters entirely.

This is a great movie for when you feel that your own zestful spirit is in danger of being crushed by jealous and fearful people. It'll encourage you to celebrate your pr-r-r-rime, and yet remember to be politic in your dealings in order to protect the integrity of your vision—and your job as a mentor.

Maggie's Morsels

Little girls! I am in the business of putting old heads on young shoulders, and all my pupils are the crème de la crème. Give me a girl at an impressionable age and she is mine for life.

★ Maggie Smith as Miss Jean Brodie
in *The Prime of Miss Jean Brodie*

I won't have to do with girls who roll up the sleeves of their blouses. We are civilized beings.

★ Maggie Smith as Miss Jean Brodie in *The Prime of Miss Jean Brodie*

Sandy, please try to do as I say and not as I do. Remember, you are a child, Sandy, and far from your prime.

★ Maggie Smith as Miss Jean Brodie in *The Prime of Miss Jean Brodie*

"I hope it will be convenient for you to see me in my office this afternoon at four-fifteen, Emily Mackay." Not four. Not four-thirty, but four-fifteen. Hmpf. She thinks to intimidate me by the use of quarter hours.

★ Maggie Smith as Miss Jean Brodie in *The Prime of Miss Jean Brodie*

You'll have to excuse me, Mr. Townsend. I have a fortuitous headache.

★ Maggie Smith as Aunt Lavinia Penniman in *Washington Square*

The Power of Two

Because where these classic creative duos are concerned, you can't have one without the other . . .

Vincent and Theo (1990)
Stars: Tim Roth, Paul Rhys
Director: Robert Altman
Writer: Julian Mitchell

This biopic of the life of Vincent van Gogh stars Tim Roth as Vincent and Paul Rhys as his compassionate and complex brother, Theo. Theo, an art dealer in Paris, supported his often broke and dangerously depressed brother, Vincent, one of the greatest painters of the nineteenth century, who sold only one painting in his life. Without Theo, who harbored and comforted Vincent when the rest of the world did not, we might never have known what a sunflower looked like in the Arlesian afternoon through Vincent's eyes.

Pollock (2000)
Stars: Ed Harris, Marcia Gay Harden, Amy Madigan
Director: Ed Harris
Writers: Barbara Turner, Susan Emshwiller, based on the book
    Jackson Pollock: An American Saga *by Steven Naifeh and*
    Gregory White Smith

This docudrama chronicles the marriage between bad boy painter Jackson Pollock (Ed Harris) and his passionate wife, Lee Krasner (Marcia Gay Harden),

. . . continued

whose tumultuous marriage painted a few pictures you'd never want to hang on a wall. Their creative collaboration, however, produced some of the most important art of the twentieth century, which was the direct result of the alchemical passion between these two gifted but tormented souls. Jackson and Lee remind us that when we join hands for better or worse, we can make history.

The Diaries of Vaslav Nijinsky (2001)
Stars: Sir Derek Jacobi, Kevin Lucas, Delia Silvan, Chris Haywood
Director: Paul Cox
Writer: Paul Cox, based on the diaries of Vaslav Nijinsky

This is a dramatization of the diaries written in the years after ballet dancer Vaslav Nijinsky's (Derek Jacobi) separation from his mentor and tor-mentor, Diaghilev (Kevin Lucas), the director of the Ballets Russes. Nijinsky's inner thoughts and tortured yet effortless movement remind us that conflict is as necessary as harmony, and that sometimes it's our enemies, or even mad-ness itself, that can bring us to new heights.

Topsy-Turvy (1999)
Stars: Allan Corduner, Dexter Fletcher, Jim Broadbent, Sukie Smith
Director and Writer: Mike Leigh

The dynamics of the creative collaboration between Gilbert and Sullivan is explored in this period pic about one of the greatest musical comedy teams in history, whose influences can still be felt today on the Great White Way. This movie chronicles the fireworks that can result when opposites attract, and reminds us all that it took discord as well as harmony to bring us *The Mikado*, just as it takes conflict as well as harmony to help us realize our full potential and make a difference in the world.

▪ *Charlotte Gray* (2001)

Stars: Cate Blanchett, Billy Crudup, Michael Gambon
Director: Gillian Armstrong
Writer: Jeremy Brock, based on the novel by Sebastian Faulks

Why does it always seem that no matter how seemingly simple and straightforward the cause—like, say, eradicating pure evil—some higher-up turns out to have ulterior motives that dishonor all your altruistic sacrifices and make you feel completely used and abused? Here's a movie that will encourage you to find your own way to fight the real battle even when others try to muck things up with their own agendas.

During World War II, Scotswoman Charlotte Gray (Cate Blanchett) is offered the opportunity to serve the Allied cause—and, in a larger sense, humankind—by risking her life to be a part of the French Resistance. This will require her to take on a false identity, speak perfectly inflected French, have secret rendezvous with anonymous contacts, and hide out with an impossibly sexy French guy named Julien Levade (Billy Crudup). Julien has a fierce determination to destroy oppression and exploitation of the common man. He also has a face with exquisite Gallic bone structure that would make for some beautiful babies. But we digress.

Charlotte manages to keep her cool even in the most dangerous of situations, calms and nurtures a couple of frightened Jewish schoolboys that Julien is hiding in the countryside, diplomatically negotiates the choppy waters of a fractured father/son relationship between Julien and his war-weary pop (Michael Gambon), and discovers that the British government has a dirty little secret. It's up to Charlotte to figure out how to stop feeling like a pawn in someone else's game, somehow genuinely make a difference in her own, small way, and fan the flames of hope for the future.

So stop worrying about what you can't change, start thinking about what you can actually do, and watch *Charlotte Gray* for a little one-woman inspiration in your own battle for what is truly important.

ᕙ

> *To bring joy to a single heart is better than to build many shrines for worship.*
> —Abu Sa'id Ibn Abi Khayr, Islamic mystic

ᕙ

Sisters Are Doing It for Themselves

Because if you want a job done right, do it yourself!

Silkwood (1983)
Stars: Meryl Streep, Cher, Kurt Russell
Director: Mike Nichols
Writers: Alice Arlen, Nora Ephron

Meryl Streep stars in the title role in this movie based on the true story of Karen Silkwood, a nuclear plant worker in Oklahoma whose friends begin suffering from the effects of radiation sickness. When she becomes contaminated, and the company won't help her, Karen takes matters into her own hands and launches a one-woman assault against the unethical practices at Kerr McGee, forcing the industry to care for its workers and take responsibility for itself. Watch this one when you're feeling like just another cog in the wheel. Let Karen's courage remind you that it's the squeaky cog that gets the grease.

Nine to Five (1980)
Stars: Jane Fonda, Lily Tomlin, Dolly Parton, Dabney Coleman
Director: Colin Higgins
Writers: Colin Higgins, Patricia Resnick, based on a story by Patricia Resnick

If you're feeling like it's just you against the world, join hands with Judy (Jane Fonda), Violet (Lily Tomlin), and Doralee (Dolly Parton), the sisters from the steno pool who take on the male-dominated corporate power structure and win, because they know that the only way to change the status quo is to stick together. If you're feeling like a slave to the machine, let these fed-up working girls remind you that sometimes a girl has to learn to say no.

. . . continued

Erin Brockovich (2000)
Stars: *Julia Roberts, Albert Finney, Aaron Eckhart, Marg Helgenberger*
Director: *Steven Soderbergh*
Writer: *Susannah Grant*

When former beauty queen turned single mom Erin Brockovich (Julia Roberts) finds herself unemployed and adrift in a world that seems indifferent to her plight, she forces a local lawyer (Albert Finney) to give her a chance as a legal claims investigator. What begins as a search for a marketable skill, however, turns into a one-woman crusade against a California power plant that has been polluting the drinking water. Erin Brockovich gathers the evidence that's necessary to force the plant to be responsible for its actions by encouraging unheard and unseen women like herself to stand up and be counted.

Dolly's Double Dips

*I have a strict policy that nobody
cries alone in my presence.*
★ Dolly Parton as Truvy in *Steel Magnolias*

Laughter through tears is my favorite emotion.
★ Dolly Parton as Truvy in *Steel Magnolias*

*Well, I always just thought if you see somebody
without a smile, give 'em yours.*
★ Dolly Parton as Miss Mona in
The Best Little Whorehouse in Texas

■ *Stowaway* (1936)
  Stars: Shirley Temple, Robert Young, Alice Faye
  Director: William A. Seiter
  Writers: William M. Conselman, Samuel G. Engel, Nat Perrin, Arthur Sheekman

Back in the Depression, Shirley Temple was rekindling feelings of hope in the hearts of people in movie theaters everywhere. Somehow, that curly-haired cutie in a short dress and patent leather Mary Janes tapped her way into people's hearts and convinced them that recovery was just around the corner and, meanwhile, why not do a happy little soft-shoe and celebrate what you've got?

Like most of the movies in the Shirley Temple oeuvre, this one finds her orphaned, which of course allows those lost souls who become enchanted by her to adopt the dimple-faced urchin—although not before several plot twists threaten her happiness and allow her a big teary scene in which she declares she will be brave, by golly, she will. In *Stowaway*, a stranger on the street, wealthy playboy Tom Randall (Robert Young), comes across Barbara "Ching-Ching" Stewart (our Shirley) in Shanghai, where she's been stranded far away from her missionary guardians and robbed in her sleep. Of course, having a purse of coins nicked is the worst that happens to Ching-Ching, because revolution, pedophilia, and exploitation of the innocent just don't exist in this corner of reality. So Shirley is magically whisked away into Tom's shipboard world, where she gets a chance to sing, dance, do vaudevillian imitations, and spout appropriate Chinese proverbs to remind everyone to be philosophical about the fickleness of fate. And of course, she also gets to look adorable in an array of silk Chinese-inspired lounging outfits.

Ching-Ching also rights all wrongs. She brings out the responsible side of a ne'er-do-well and the adventurous side of a woman who is afraid to break up with her coldhearted fiancé. The rich learn that money isn't everything and they begin to spread the wealth, the greedy lose that which they most want to possess, and the poor are rescued from poverty. Yes, the spirited, talented, and relentlessly optimistic Shirley not only heals troubled souls, she single-handedly creates a system of economic parity within free-market capitalism. Quick, somebody elect that girl president!

When you need an infusion of positivity to fuel your daily struggles to keep your sunny side up, indulge in a rainy day matinee of *Stowaway* and remember to S-M-I-L-E.

When one has made up his mind to go to a certain place, his feet function without any mental activity.

—Vasishtha

■ **Death to Smoochy** (2002)
Stars: *Robin Williams, Edward Norton, Catherine Keener, Jon Stewart, Danny DeVito*
Director: *Danny DeVito*
Writer: *Adam Resnick*

"You can't change the world, but you can make a dent" is the motto of Sheldon Mopes (Edward Norton), a fellow who is far more energetic and optimistic than his name suggests. Sheldon's alter-ego is Smoochy the Rhino, a Barney-esque creature that teaches children about love, understanding, and the importance of eating plenty of organic whole-grain foods. Sheldon is slightly down on his luck when Kidnet executive and re-formed kiddie host groupie Nora Wells (Catherine Keener) tracks him down, but he's relentlessly cheery throughout his regular gig at the Coney Island methadone clinic, even if his audience is a bunch of fellas in parkas who keep nodding off. And Sheldon is elated to discover that Nora and her boss, Stokes (Jon Stewart), are tapping him to replace the time slot formerly occupied by the scandal-ridden "Rainbow" Randolph Smiley (Robin Williams). Finally, a chance for the idealistic, Buddha-like Sheldon to inspire children everywhere!

Alas, Sheldon is the proverbial babe in the woods, ignorant of the elaborate profit-generating machine of children's television. Before you can say "Soy dogs for everyone! With extra spirulina sauce!" Sheldon has made enemies all around—and he's still got the maniacal, vengeful "Rainbow" Randolph out to get him. Can one guileless man with a gentle soul, who can find childlike joy in anyone and anything—including a dildo-shaped cookie—find the power to stand up to the enemies of innocence?

When you're feeling like the lone voice of optimism in a chorus of cynical profiteers, this edgy black comedy will have you believing that you too can discover your personal power, maintain creative control, and triumph against the forces of greed—all without resorting to the use of toxic and inorganic substances.

The World According to Smoochy

Look, don't get me wrong, okay? I mean, I'm not literally comparing Captain Kangaroo to Jesus Christ. I'm just saying that the Captain, like Christ, was someone that, you know, you could really, really believe in. You know, with those guys it wasn't about all the bells and the whistles and the ricketa racketa. It was all about the work. Especially Jesus. I mean, forget about it!

★ Edward Norton as Sheldon Mopes in *Death to Smoochy*

I will not encourage children to consume endless amounts of refined sugar. I have to wake up in the morning and live with myself.

★ Edward Norton as Sheldon Mopes in *Death to Smoochy*

He slams the door/he stomps his feet/he sends me to bed with zilch to eat/but my stepdad's not mad/he's just adjusting.

★ Edward Norton as Sheldon Mopes in *Death to Smoochy*

▪ *12 Angry Men* (1957)
Stars: *Henry Fonda, Jack Klugman, Lee J. Cobb, Ed Begley, E. G. Marshall,*
  Jack Warden, Martin Balsam, John Savoca
Director: *Sidney Lumet*
Writer: *Reginald Rose*

This classic courtroom drama set in a claustrophobic jury room shows just how hard it can be for a poor man of color to achieve justice when a "jury of his peers" consists of twelve white men locked in a tiny room on a muggy summer day with a broken fan. And unbeknownst to the defendant (John Savoca), he comes within a whisper of being found guilty and sentenced to death in less time than it takes to open a window, take off a jacket, and check your watch. Luckily, one man—juror number eight (Henry Fonda)—isn't willing to ditch his duty for a quick escape to a cool office.

Despite his fellow jurors' flaring tempers, racist speeches, and contempt for logic and facts, juror number eight insists on exploring the evidence and testimony in further detail. As the afternoon wears on and one man grouses about missing tonight's Yankees' game and another declares that these "tough kids should be slapped down before they get into trouble," one by one, inspired by juror number eight, each man tentatively brings up a point about the case that speaks to his own experience. Can the men put aside their impatience and bigotry and use their personal resources to bring the truth to the surface? Or are a couple of ball game tickets and the desperate need for a cold drink and a working source of cool air going to send this kid to the chair?

When you're feeling like the odd one out, under pressure to cave in to the majority, this movie's a refreshing reminder that democracy doesn't mean decision by bullying and intimidation, and that if you have the courage to act from your conscience, you might be able to get through to even the most stubborn of minds.

Chapter 8

All That Glitters Isn't Gold: Keeping It Real Movies

Are you waiting to see your name in lights but somebody keeps pulling the plug? Is the stretch limousine of your celebrity stuck in gridlock? If you're sick and tired of waiting around for your fifteen minutes, and need a comforting reminder that maybe fame isn't all that it's cracked up to be, watch one of these Keeping It Real Movies about starlets just like you and me who learn that all that glitters isn't gold. They'll help you realize that the spotlight isn't all it's cracked up to be, and that there's no star treatment in the world that can compare with the love of your family and friends.

■ *Chicago* (2002)
Stars: Catherine Zeta-Jones, Renée Zellweger, Richard Gere
Director: Rob Marshall
Writer: Bill Condon, based on the play by Maurine Dallas Watkins and the
  musical by Bob Fosse and Fred Ebb

Granted, a noisy hall where there's a nightly brawl might seem like an unlikely place to go to rekindle the hearth fires of home. But Bob Fosse's cynical, sensual homage to that infamous city of jazz and gin is one of the toe tappingest morality tales ever performed on the deck of a sinking ship, and reminds us of how far off the path we can wander when we've got stars in our eyes.

When ambitious and amoral cabaret chanteuse Roxie Hart (Renée Zellweger) tries to sleep her way to the top but winds up without star billing, she shoots her lying lothario in cold blood, gets caught, and goes on trial for her life. What actually goes on trial in Chicago, however, isn't Roxie at all, or even the conscienceless double murderess Velma (Catherine Zeta-Jones), but rather our celebrity-driven culture, where fame and infamy are interchangeable, and where everything, even the justice system, becomes a cabaret act where the person with the most razzle-dazzle wins.

This is a great movie to watch when the shadows of obscurity are closing in on your personal speakeasy. *Chicago* reminds us that whether we're in Chi-Town or Philly or Ashtabula or even Timbuktu, we need to focus on the light within and keep the home fires burning.

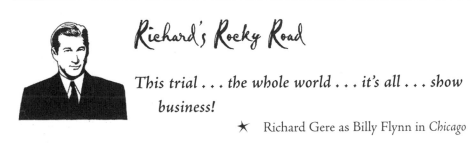

Richard's Rocky Road

This trial . . . the whole world . . . it's all . . . show business!

★ Richard Gere as Billy Flynn in *Chicago*

. . . continued

They'd love you a lot more if you were hanged! You know why?
Because it would sell more papers. . . .That's Chicago!
★ Richard Gere as Billy Flynn in *Chicago*

Would you please tell the audience . . . err . . . the jury what
happened?
★ Richard Gere as Billy Flynn in *Chicago*

Give 'em the old razzle-dazzle. Razzle-dazzle 'em. Give 'em an
act with lots of flash in it and the reaction will be passionate.
★ Richard Gere as Billy Flynn in *Chicago*

■ *To Die For* (1995)
Stars: *Nicole Kidman, Joaquin Phoenix, Matt Dillon, Illeana Douglas, Dan Hedaya*
Director: *Gus Van Sant*
Writer: *Buck Henry, based on the book by Joyce Maynard*

If you're feeling frustrated in your pursuit of fame and fortune, let Suzanne Stone Maretto, the up-and-comer from hell, help you readjust your priorities. Nicole Kidman stars as Suzanne, a vapidly beautiful everywoman who elevates coordinating separates to the level of the divine, and for whom national events, world leaders, war, peace, and even the weather are just props in her bid for fame. And if national leaders and matters of state are mere instruments in her rise to the top, imagine how Suzanne must feel about her meddling in-laws and her guileless and relaxed-fit hubby (Matt Dillon), whose plans for Suzanne include a mom-and-pop café, a passel of kids, and Suzanne leaving her dreams behind. Unfortunately, Suzanne learns too late that the thin ice of celebrity is poised just a few short inches away from the cold depths of obscurity.

Nicole's Nougats

You aren't really anybody in America if you're not on TV.

★ Nicole Kidman as Suzanne Stone Maretto in *To Die For*

The French are glad to die for love. They delight in fighting duels. But I prefer a man who lives . . . and gives expensive . . . jewels.

★ Nicole Kidman as Satine in *Moulin Rouge!*

I'm rather ashamed of my plans. I make a new one every day.

★ Nicole Kidman as Isabel Archer in *Portrait of a Lady*

But if it is a choice between Richmond and death, I choose death.

★ Nicole Kidman as Virginia Woolf in *The Hours*

Oh, we could give it a try. I'll bring the wine, you bring your scarred psyche.

★ Nicole Kidman as Dr. Chase Meridian in *Batman Forever*

Control is an illusion, you infantile egomaniac. Nobody knows what's gonna happen next: not on a freeway, not in an airplane, not inside our own bodies, and certainly not on a racetrack with forty other infantile egomaniacs.

★ Nicole Kidman as Dr. Claire Lewicki in *Days of Thunder*

Bitch Goddesses

They drummed you out of Hollywood, so you come crawling back to Broadway. But Broadway doesn't go for booze and dope. Now get out of my way, I've got a man waiting for me.

★ Susan Hayward as Helen Lawson in *Valley of the Dolls*

Honey, we see everything in this profession, but one thing I ain't never seen—man or woman—is a grown-up.

★ Theresa Merritt as Jewel in *The Best Little Whorehouse in Texas*

Maybe I don't want to meet someone who shares my interests. I hate my interests.

★ Steve Buscemi as Seymour in *Ghost World*

■ **Valley of the Dolls** (1967)
Stars: Patty Duke, Barbara Parkins, Sharon Tate, Tony Scotti
Director: Mark Robson
Writers: Helen Deutsch, Dorothy Kingsley, Jacqueline Susann,
 based on the novel by Jacqueline Susann

Three well-scrubbed, multitalented, and ambitious young women come to the Big Apple in search of fame and fortune and wind up hitting the big time. They also wind up hitting the booze, the pills, and the Aqua Net with reckless abandon, which results not only in a Judy Garland–scale substance abuse problem, but the worst set of bubble-dos this side of *Gidget Goes Hawaiian*.

There's Neely (Patty Duke), the young singing sensation who climbs to the top of the heap only to topple into the abyss of egomania; she also has really lousy taste in men. There's Anne (Barbara Parkins), the wholesome girl next door who scales the heights of the fashion world, only to plummet into the depths of despair because she can't get her guy to say "I do." And finally there's Jennifer (Sharon Tate), who tops Hollywood's A-list only to wind up doing soft porn for a C-grade French smut merchant to fund her husband, Tony's (Tony Scotti), extended stay in the loony bin—the same loony bin, in fact, where Neely is detoxing, which is convenient, as it provides an opportunity for Neely and Tony to belt out an old ballad or two together and send us all running for the blessed silence of obscurity.

In the end, all of us dolls learn that the peaks of celebrity are ringed 'round by the treacherous valleys of low self-esteem, bad relationships, and quality pharmaceuticals, and the only hope we all have for enduring happiness is to come down out of the highlands and embrace a more grounded life on the plains.

Peppermint Pattys

I have to get up at five o'clock in the morning and
SPARKLE, Neely, SPARKLE!
★ Patty Duke as Neely O'Hara in *Valley of the Dolls*

Boobies, boobies, boobies. Nothin' but boobies.
Who needs 'em?
★ Patty Duke as Neely O'Hara in *Valley of the Dolls*

I didn't have dough handed to me because of my good cheekbones, I
had to earn it.
★ Patty Duke as Neely O'Hara in *Valley of the Dolls*

Bev's Culinarytherapy: Humble Pie

When the air is getting thin on your lofty peak and you're hungry for the down-to-earth taste of home, try this recipe for Humble Pie and savor the simplicity.

Here's what you'll need:

1 12-ounce can Pillsbury
    Big Country Refrigerated
    Buttermilk Biscuits
3 tablespoons butter
1 onion, diced
1 green bell pepper, seeded
    and diced

1 pound lean ground beef
1 can chicken gumbo or
    cream of chicken soup
Monterey Jack cheese, grated

Here's how you do it:

 Grease a 9 x 12-inch baking pan. Separate the biscuits and arrange them on the bottom of the pan. Pat them down so they cover the entire bottom of the pan, because, as we all know, every great humble pie begins with a solid foundation. In a medium skillet, melt the butter, add the onion and green pepper, and sauté until soft. Add the ground beef, brown, and drain. Add the chicken soup to the ground beef mixture, return to the heat, and simmer on low until the whole mess gets soupy, then pour it over the unbaked biscuits. Top with the grated cheese and bake in a 350°F oven until done, then eat the whole pan in a hurry before it congeals. This dish is guaranteed to keep you firmly rooted in the earth for about eight to twelve hours.

▪ *Lisa Picard Is Famous* (2000)
Stars: Laura Kirk, Nat DeWolf
Director: Griffin Dunne
Writers: Nat DeWolf, Laura Kirk

If you've been feeling passed over in the casting call of love, this movie about a fledgling actress's search for the spotlight will remind you what you really need to feel like a star isn't fame, but the love and devotion of a best friend.

This mockumentary begins as an investigation into the transformative power of celebrity, and takes as its subject a young woman apparently on the verge of stardom. The film follows her through the months preceding her big break on a made-for-TV movie starring Melissa Gilbert.

As we watch Lisa (Laura Kirk) dashing to auditions, harassing her agent, and most important, hanging out with her best friend, Tate (Nat DeWolf), the filmmaker wonders, will fame change the way Lisa walks? Will fame change the way Lisa talks? Will her agent finally start to return her calls? And will she still breathe exclusively through her left nostril for twenty minutes before every audition? In other words, what will change when Lisa's name is finally up in lights?

And the answer is, a lot. Most notably, her relationship with her soul mate, Tate, begins to dim as Lisa's star rises and her life in front of the camera begins to overwhelm her connection to the sources of her real strength. And when Lisa's star starts to run out of gas before reaching supernova, we realize right along with her that there is no fame as fulfilling as the love of a best friend, and the only accolades that matter are the love and appreciation that you see in the eyes of your loved ones.

Nancy's Momentous Minutiae: "Gentle Hearts"

Audrey Hepburn was distressed by having to toss a cat out of a cab and into the street in *Breakfast at Tiffany's*.

The production company responsible for the movie *The Adventures of Ford Fairlane* had to reassure protestors who were upset that a classic 1957 Ford Fairlane was not blown up for the film—it was a fake.

The original ending of the Rankin and Bass classic Christmas movie *Rudolph the Red-Nosed Reindeer* was changed after angry protest letters arrived, demanding that the poor toys stuck on the Island of Misfit Toys be rescued by Santa and taken to good homes.

■ *Mystery Men* (1999)
Stars: *William H. Macy, Ben Stiller, Janeane Garofalo, Hank Azaria, Greg Kinnear, Kel Mitchell, Paul Reubens, Geoffrey Rush, Louise Lasser*
Director: *Kinka Usher*
Writer: *Neil Cuthbert, based on the comic book series* Dark Horse *by Bob Burden*

Feeling that you'll never get the public recognition that you deserve? Here's some reassurance that your inner Wonder Woman will have her moment in the sun—and when she does, don't be surprised if it's anticlimactic compared to the joy you've found just by doing the right thing in your own unique way.

Eddie, aka The Shoveler (William H. Macy), is a part-time superhero and the leader of a ragtag cadre that never quite makes it into the limelight, thanks to the superior efforts and PR placement of the well-merchandised Captain Amazing (Greg Kinnear). Captain Amazing has more corporate sponsors than all the Nascar drivers combined, but he also possesses an ego the size of a bloated Hollywood budget green-lighted by guys who get carried away with pyrotechnics, gadgets, and chase scenes. Hence, he manages to get himself kidnapped by the evil Casanova Frankenstein (Geoffrey Rush), giving Eddie and his pals their big chance to prove they've got the right stuff.

And so The Blue Rajah (Hank Azaria) pilfers some of his mom's (Louise Lasser) silverware for weapons, Mr. Furious (Ben Stiller) gets in touch with the power of his inner rage, The Spleen (Paul Reubens) readies his weapons of gastrointestinal destruction, The Invisible Boy (Kel Mitchell) leaves his preoccupied parents at home, and The Bowler (Janeane Garofalo) arms herself with a skull-embedded bowling ball and an endless string of snarky comments. Along with The Shoveler, they set off to save their city and the hapless Captain Amazing. And because this is a comic-book world, of course they succeed.

So if you're having one of those days when it just seems that the world is overlooking your magnificence, have a laugh with *Mystery Men* and reassure yourself that fighting the good fight is the real reward.

The meek shall inherit the earth.

—Psalm 37:11

Skin Deep

Your soul can't soar when you're weighted down with obsessions about the body it's housed in. Obsessed with your insecurities, your failings, and your dress size? These flicks are great reminders that focusing on your face and figure will blind you to how lovely and amazing you really are.

A Woman's Face *(1941)*
Stars: Joan Crawford, Melvyn Douglas, Conrad Veidt, Reginald Owen,
   Richard Nichols
Director: George Cukor
Writers: Donald Ogden Stewart, Elliot Paul, based on the play
   Il Était Une Fois by Francis De Croisset

Anna Holm (Joan Crawford) does a good job of staying in the shadows and wearing huge stylish hats at severe angles, but while her film noir poses hide the ghastly scars on her face, they don't do much for her self-acceptance. Convinced the world despises her because of her disfigurement—caused when her drunken father set their home on fire when she was a child—Anna has chosen to despise the world right back. Yes, Anna has become leader of her very own gang of criminals whose specialty is blackmailing the beautiful people.

Fortunately, a surgeon (Melvyn Douglas) kindly fixes her face for free, and when the bandages come off, Anna is indeed a flawless beauty. But she's also deeply unsettled. Now that she doesn't feel like a monster, what's a girl to do? Does she behave like the nasty piece of work she always thought she was? After all, she *is* committed to helping carry out her sociopathic

. . . continued

boyfriend's (Conrad Veidt) latest scheme to murder some unfortunate little rich boy, and a gal really ought to follow through on her promises. Or should she accept that the mirror now accurately reflects her higher self, and begin living out her secret dream of a happy, simple life with a man who embraces her light as well as her shadow?

Okay, so things get campy when Anna bitch-slaps her blackmail victim, and there's something really creepy about Joan Crawford's starry-eyed speech declaring her desire to be just a wife and mom, given her Mommie Dearest reputation. But if you find yourself thinking all your problems would be solved if you just had a Hollywood lighting technician following you everywhere 24/7, check out *A Woman's Face* and remember that it's a megawatt inner light that will truly make you glow like a movie star.

So Nice They Did It Twice: Ingrid Bergman originally brought *A Woman's Face* to the screen in 1938 when she was a star in Sweden and could get scripts green-lighted, but the original's emphasis on running away from your past and repressing your dark side is far less satisfying than the don't-hate-me-just-because-I'm-evil-incarnate Joan Crawford version.

Lovely and Amazing (2001)
Stars: Brenda Blethyn, Catherine Keener, Emily Mortimer,
  Raven Goodwin, Dermot Mulroney, Jake Gyllenhaal
Director and Writer: Nicole Holofcener

Mom Jane Marks (Brenda Blethyn) truly believes that her three daughters are lovely and amazing creatures. Unfortunately, for all the unconditional love she's given them, Jane has also been a role model for vain neurosis at times, and all of her girls have inherited her tendency to equate their self-worth with how other people see them. Thus, Elizabeth (Emily Mortimer), an actress, and little Annie (Raven Goodwin), Jane's adopted child, are convinced that if

. . . continued

they only had toned upper arms or straight hair their insecurities and feelings of abandonment would magically disappear. Flippant Michelle (Catherine Keener) is living on the laurels of having been homecoming queen more than a decade ago, but deep down she fears that being nothing more than a wife and mom who fashions fussy crafts that no one appreciates makes her inconsequential and pitiful. As their mother tries to recover from a painful and expensive liposuction surgery, all three daughters struggle to put aside their obsessions and neuroses and reconnect with the part of themselves that loves and is loved regardless of how fabulous they seem at a cocktail party.

Watch this one when you need a reminder that you are not your flabby upper arms—or when you need to have a good laugh at your own tendency to spiral inward in self-loathing—and see if it doesn't pull you out of your funk.

Beautiful (2000)
Stars: Minnie Driver, Joey Lauren Adams, Hallie Kate Eisenberg, Kathleen Turner, Colleen Rennison, Linda Hart
Director: Sally Field
Writer: Jon Bernstein

In this bittersweet spoof of a maniacally ambitious beauty queen, the contrast between two daughters, each born with the same admirable and lovable qualities but raised by very different mothers, shows us the power of unconditional love to water the seeds of inner beauty.

As a little girl, spunky and ambitious Mona (Colleen Rennison) starts a grocery delivery service to finance her participation in every junior missy beauty pageant in the county. She's able to overcome frizzy brown hair and crooked teeth and even devises her own way to ward off a leering stepfather, yet her mother is completely unsupportive and condescending toward her and her dreams. Mona's desperate need for love causes her to confuse outer beauty

. . . continued

with inner grace and turns her into a downright insufferable adult (played by Minnie Driver) driven to win that national crown by any means necessary—including doing an interpretive jazz dance routine to "Bicycle Built for Two" while twirling fire batons.

Machiavellian Mona hardly seems to deserve her endlessly supportive friend, Ruby (Joey Lauren Adams), whose adoptive daughter, Vanessa (Hallie Kate Eisenberg), has all the lovely qualities Mona had as a child, including forthrightness: Vanessa openly loathes the shallow Mona. Vanessa, however, has the advantage of a loving mother who nurtures her soul, and ultimately this allows her to show the kind of compassion and love toward Mona that even Mona's adult mother (Linda Hart) can't muster. Vanessa's grace teaches Mona the meaning of true beauty.

Watch this one when you're feeling beastly and see if it doesn't remind you of the beauty within, which has no need of a sparkly tiara, a satin sash, or outside validation.

Real Women Have Curves (2002)
Stars: America Ferrera, Lupe Ontiveros, Ingrid Oliu
Director: Patricia Cardoso
Writers: Josefina Lopez, George LaVoo, based on the play by
*   Josefina Lopez*

This is an empowering movie about a girl with a healthy sense of entitlement, who daily has to fend off spirit-squelching criticism about her looks from Mama. Teenage Ana (America Ferrera) may be stuck in a run-down section of L.A., but her life is shaping up to be much better than that of her mother (Lupe Ontiveros), who had to quit school and begin working at age thirteen. Ana is smart enough to see through her mother's taking-to-her-bed

. . . continued

histrionics and cruel jibes at Ana's weight—that's just Mama's deep-rooted jealousy speaking.

She's no size two, or even a size twelve, but she's not about to let anyone make her feel small. Ana refuses to diet or feel bad about herself or her body—and she secretly fills out college applications even as she starts working in her sister Estela's (Ingrid Oliu) sweatshop. Ana isn't sure what bothers her more: her sister's refusal to demand higher pay from the buyer who takes advantage of her dress-designing talents and hard work, or spending summer days steam-ironing ball gowns in a stuffy room.

Inspired by a clingy, sexy red dress her sister designed and sewed for her in her rare spare moments, Ana decides to unleash a revolution. She rallies her sister and fellow workers to cast off their outer garments as well as their feelings of inadaquacy, make peace with their cellulite, and remember that real women have curves . . . and minds . . . and a right to determine their own destiny.

Pop this one in when you need a shot of encouragement to tune out the naysayers. Then love and honor yourself just as you are.

Chapter 9

My Karma Ran Over My Dogma: Letting Go of Your Status Quo Movies

So you've been cruising down the highway of life past the signposts that reassure you that you're on your way. Suddenly, you realize that you've been misreading your map, you have no idea where you are, and worse, your karma has made roadkill of your dogma.

When visibility has dropped dangerously low and the old credos aren't working anymore, you need one of these Letting Go of Your Status Quo Movies to clarify your view. They'll remind you that when you double back and consider new directions, you may find an even better road to travel.

- ***Toy Story*** *(1995)*
  Stars: *The voices of Tom Hanks, Tim Allen, Don Rickles, John Morris,*
      Erik von Detten, Laurie Metcalf
  Director: *John Lasseter*
  Writers: *Joss Whedon, Andrew Stanton, Joel Cohen, Alec Sokolow,*
      based on a story by John Lasseter, Andrew Stanton, Peter Docter, Joe Ranft

It's not every day you find echoes of Dante's *Divine Comedy* in a kids' movie, but this animated feature, packed with pop culture references, is one of the finest journey-to-hell-and-back movies we've ever seen.

Cowboy Woody (Tom Hanks) is the amiable leader of the toys belonging to a boy named Andy (John Morris). Woody feels perfectly secure in his position—why, he could organize plastic corrosion awareness meetings in his sleep, he's so good at running things. And he's ever-reassuring to the other toys that no one's going to be next month's garage sale fodder, even though Andy's birthday party is coming up and he's sure to get some new toys that will change the dynamic in the room.

But Woody's world is turned upside down when his beloved Andy transfers his loyalties to his new action figure—Buzz Lightyear (Tim Allen), whose ultramodern whistles, bells, and laser beams put poor Woody's "Howdy, Partner" drawstring mechanism to shame. Suddenly, Buzz occupies the sacred ground on Andy's bed, and worse, this interloper believes his own packaging—Buzz actually thinks he's a space ranger who can go "To infinity and beyond!"

Disgusted and deeply envious, Woody hatches a dark plan for revenge. But the whole thing goes horribly awry, and before Woody knows it, both he and Buzz are spiritually lost, wandering through circles of hell and facing Satan himself—namely, that destructive little brat next door (Erik von Detten) who keeps torturing his toys. Alas, Woody must redeem himself and Buzz must accept his true nature if they are ever to return home to the gentle land of Mr. Potato Head, Slinky the Dog, and Andy's love.

Feeling displaced? Have a laugh with *Toy Story* and remember that if you can let go of fear, distrust, and ego attachment, you might not get back to the paradise you lost but you may well find a new one that's even more delightful.

❦

*In the middle of the journey of our life I came to myself within a
dark wood where the straight way was lost.*

—Dante, "The Inferno," canto 1, 1.1, from *The Divine Comedy*

❦

■ *Born on the Fourth of July* (1989)
Stars: Tom Cruise, Willem Dafoe, Kyra Sedgwick, Raymond J. Barry
Director: Oliver Stone
Writers: Oliver Stone, Ron Kovic, based on the book by Ron Kovic

This true story of a disillusioned Vietnam vet is a classic case of a man whose karma ran over his dogma, leaving him with no goals, no education, no career, and no place to go but up.

As a kid in Long Island, Ron (Tom Cruise) is a typical early sixties boys' boy, playing cowboys and Indians in the woods and waving a little flag at the Fourth of July small-town parade. Caught up in idealism about his country, he joins the army and before you can say "Be careful what you wish for" he's in Vietnam fighting for truth, justice, the American way—and his family's and community's approval. And yes, he does end up getting the parade and the applause and the misty-eyed looks. But despite his local-hero brave face, Ron's self-concept is as shattered as his illusions about the glory and grandeur of war. Can he reclaim his heroic and altruistic self and find a way to express it? After all, we'd like to believe he's got the potential to do far more daring things than swallow the worm in a bottle of tequila.

Watch this one when your road is blocked and your map isn't working for you. It just may inspire you to stick the old map in the glove compartment and seek an alternative route.

❦

*New every morning is the love/Our wakening and uprising
prove/Through sleep and darkness safely brought,/Restored to
life, and power, and thought.*

—from the hymn "New Every Morning Is the Love"

❦

■ *Tortilla Soup* (2001)

> Stars: Hector Elizondo, Elizabeth Peña, Jaqueline Obradors, Tamara Mello,
>   Paul Rodriguez, Raquel Welch
> Director: María Ripoll
> Writers: Ramón Menéndez, Tom Musca, Vera Blasi, based on the screenplay
>   Eat Drink Man Woman *by Hui-Ling Wang, Ang Lee, James Schamus*

Finding that the same old, same old isn't working for you and yours anymore but afraid to move on? *Tortilla Soup* dishes up a heaping lesson in how you can find enrichment and joy by changing your perspective, your assumptions—and your dinner guest list.

Widowed chef Martin Naranjo (Hector Elizondo) and his three daughters have been eating Sunday dinner together since forever, bonding over a multicourse feast that makes the casual observer wonder how they could possibly own enough Tupperware to store all the leftovers. Maybe it's time to consider halving the recipes, especially since all three girls are secretly itching to have tables of their own and start new traditions. Sure, they all love each other very much, but no one quite trusts that if the menu changes and the seating chart gets adjusted each week, her loving connections will be maintained.

So they start to play musical chairs, tentatively seeking independence and blaming each other for being the one who has upset the pot. Carmen (Jaqueline Obradors) commits to buying a condo, Maribel (Tamara Mello) impulsively decides to move in with her new boyfriend, and Leticia (Elizabeth Peña), the one who seriously considered the convent, actually smiles at a good-looking man (Paul Rodriguez). And unbeknownst to them all, Dad too has found new sources of love and new friends to try out his recipes on. Can they still break bread—or tortillas—without giving in to resentments and accusations of disloyalty?

When you have a taste for change but are hesitant to try a new recipe, watch *Tortilla Soup* and be inspired to break a few rules and a few dishes.

Bev's Culinarytherapy: Tortilla Soup

When you're feeling cold and hungry, do what they do when winter comes to the high-country desert, and put a pot of tortilla soup on the stove to simmer while you contemplate the coming of spring.

Here's what you'll need:

3 cups diced pork
Flour for dredging
 (approx. ½ cup)
2 cups chicken stock
6 roasted Anaheim peppers
2 roasted jalapeño peppers
2 cloves garlic, crushed
1 diced tomato
Dash cilantro, sage, and
 oregano
½ teaspoon crushed, dried
 red pepper

1 cup dried hominy or 3 cups
 fresh posole (available at
 Latin specialty grocers)
Salt and pepper
Juice of 1 lime
½ cup flour
Tortilla chips
Grated cheese, preferably
 Monterey Jack

Here's how you do it:

Dredge the pork in flour, coating the cubes on all sides. Place the dredged cubes, along with the remainder of the flour, in a dry, hot stockpot. Stir the pork and the flour constantly, until the flour toasts to a golden brown.

. . . continued

Add 2 cups of the chicken stock and stir the roux until it's smooth.

Pull the peppers into thin strips, toss with salt and crushed garlic, and add to the simmering chicken stock, along with tomatoes. Next, add cilantro, sage, and oregano, as well as the crushed red pepper, hominy (or fresh posole if you can), and pepper.

Simmer the stew for 1½ hours on low heat, until the posole is soft and the pork is tender. Before serving, toss some crushed tortilla chips and a little grated cheese on top. Then call a tribal council meeting, dish up your tortilla soup, and commune with the elders.

 Warning Label: *When Peter Piper picked a peck of pickled peppers, he was wearing rubber gloves and kept his hands away from his eyes.*

Nothing endures but change.

—Heraclitus

 ## Can I Get That Printed on a Coffee Mug?

I don't know where we're goin', but there's no sense bein' late.

★ Tom Selleck as Matthew Quigley in *Quigley Down Under*

■ *Rock Star* (2001)
Stars: Mark Wahlberg, Jennifer Aniston, Timothy Olyphant, Jason Flemyng
Director: Stephen Herek
Writer: John Stockwell

Even when others think our lives our enviable, we may find ourselves wondering whether our happiness is live or just Memorex.

Mark Wahlberg plays Chris Cole, a copy machine repairman from Pittsburgh who has found his life's fulfillment singing his favorite songs in a tribute band that imitates his heroes, the heavy metal band Steel Dragon. Oh, others may scoff at his histrionic delivery, careful application of concealer and mascara, and perfectionist mastery of his hero's vocal nuances, given that he generally sings to a roomful of metalheads who wouldn't know a head voice from a head on a mug of Budweiser. But Chris is totally devoted to his craft. No wonder his dream comes true and the real Steel Dragon calls to ask if he'll audition to replace their lead singer (Jason Flemyng), who has stormed off in a fit of pique.

This turn of events thrills and astonishes Chris and his self-possessed girlfriend, Emily (Jennifer Aniston), a stylish gal with an uncanny knack for being a good two decades ahead of the times in fashion sense, piercings, and colloquialisms. Don't you just love when they can't get the historical details right even when the filmmakers obviously lived through the era? Mandarin cosmopolitans in eighties L.A.? Baby-blue eyeliner? Uh-huh.

So Chris and Emily get to live the genuine rock-and-roll life. In other words, he renames himself Izzy and gets laid and drunk a lot and she, bored by the orgy scene, gets stuck with the other girlfriends backstage watching every big-haired, stilettoed, leather-miniskirted babe in a thirty-mile radius hit on her man. Somehow, this is not what they bargained for.

Rock Star is a fun flick to watch when you're feeling guilty for being unhappy with the trappings of success. Because regardless of what others think, you're the one who has to choose the next song on your set list. And hey, if you want to chuck it all and start over at open-mike night, we say: Go for it.

⌇

The first key to wisdom is assiduous and frequent questioning. . . .
For by doubting we come to inquiry, and by inquiry we arrive
at truth.

—Abelard

⌇

▪ *Inherit the Wind* (1960)
  Stars: Spencer Tracy, Fredric March, Gene Kelly, Dick York
  Director: Stanley Kramer
  Writers: Nedrick Young, Harold Jacob Smith, based on the play by Jerome Lawrence
    and Robert E. Lee

Based on the Scopes "Monkey" trial of 1925, this movie casts blind faith against reason, fear against trust, and xenophobia against acceptance, and shows that if we have the courage to open our minds to new realities, we will find true faith and maintain our connection to something larger than ourselves.

In the little town of Hillsboro, Alabama, schoolteacher Bertram Cates (Dick York) stands accused of teaching evolution in a public high school, which is against state law. The ensuing trial captures the imagination of the entire country and soon the town is swarming with reporters, protestors, and carnival barkers creating a circuslike atmosphere.

Prosecuting Cates is Matthew Brady (Fredric March), a stodgy old man whose claims to fame are two failed runs for president, the ability to quote scripture that applies to any occasion, and a pompous streak as wide as the Mississippi. Defending Cates is Brady's old pal Henry Drummond (Spencer Tracy), a well-known lawyer from Chicago who has a regular-joe attitude, a powerful sense of ethics—and an annoying sidekick named E. K. Hornbeck (Gene Kelly), who represents the worst attributes of the established New York elite that looks down on regular folks. Then again, Hornbeck's contempt is understandable given that the locals are prone to burning in effigy anyone whom they suspect of being less than God-fearing, marching around singing "We Will Hang Henry Drummond from a

Sour Apple Tree" to the tune of "The Battle Hymn of the Republic," and carrying picket signs that say KEEP SATAN OUT OF HILLSBORO.

Over the summer, in a blistering hot courtroom, the trial becomes less about the right to teach evolution than about the right of man to let go of fear and use his God-given ability to reason. Only if man embraces this gift, warns Drummond, can humankind progress and knowledge grow.

Watch this one when other people's fear and suspicions have you feeling stifled and claustrophobic and you need an infusion of the cool, bracing air of free thinking.

Matthew Brady (Fredric March): There used to be a mutuality of understanding and admiration between us, Henry. Why is it, my old friend, that you've moved so far away from me?
Henry Drummond (Spencer Tracy): Well, all motion is relative, Matt. Maybe it's you who have moved away—by standing still.

★ from *Inherit the Wind*

■ *Alice* (1990)
Stars: Mia Farrow, Joe Mantegna, William Hurt, Alec Baldwin, Keye Luke
Director and Writer: Woody Allen

Alice (Mia Farrow) doesn't spend much time pondering her status quo because she's distracted by the grueling demands of her day: You know, the typical wife-and-mom stuff like scheduling masseuse appointments, coping with free-range chicken shortages, and selecting a kindergarten that will offer her son the best chance of eventually getting into an

Ivy League school. But despite surface appearances, Alice also has deep longings of the soul, and a secret desire to work with Mother Teresa that she has been repressing for far too long. Afraid to explore the conflict between her values and her daily priorities, Alice mistakenly thinks that her biggest problem is inexplicable back pain. It doesn't occur to her that she's sleepwalking through her own life. Heck, she doesn't even notice that her husband (William Hurt)—who ridicules her musings about possibly just maybe stretching her wings and exploring her talents—is always working late but never answers his phone when she calls the office.

On the advice of friends, Alice visits Dr. Yang (Keye Luke), a mysterious acupuncturist who prescribes horrible-tasting herbal teas that apparently can cure anything from chronic pain to existential alienation. Soon Alice starts to wake up, see more clearly, and discover mysterious, hidden powers: the ability to seduce handsome sax players (Joe Mantegna) and figure out what her friends really think of her. Yep, by the time she flies over Manhattan in the moonlight hand in hand with the ghost of a sexy ex-lover (Alec Baldwin), you too might start feeling the urge to wander the little side streets in Chinatown to find Dr. Yang's exact address.

Even if you don't have the advantage of magical realism as a plot device in your personal narrative, this movie will remind you that taking a fresh look at your life from a new vantage point may just give you the courage to acknowledge your heart's desire and to venture forth to fulfill it.

∽

The hard and stiff are followers of death. The gentle and soft are the followers of life.

—Tao Te Ching

∽

Playing God

When it comes to portraying God on-screen, it seems that moviemakers resort to high-concept casting, over-the-top reverence, outrageous irreverence, or some sort of touchy-feely white aura that feels decidedly nondenominational. Here are some of our favorite ways that moviemakers have chosen to portray the divine force.

The Ten Commandments (1956)

It's God in all his Vista Vision, Cecil B. DeMille glory! God first appears to Moses as a "burning bush": a Charlie Brown Christmas–type tree surrounded by a pulsating orange aura, speaking in a deep bass voice, accompanied by organ chords. God also appears as a swirl of white stars that turns into a pillar of fire, all the better to sear commandments into stone on a mountainside, creating the tablets. And contrary to popular belief, God, also known as "I Am," was not that bright green fog that creeps through the land of Egypt causing firstborn sons to collapse and drop dead at Ramses's feet—that was that nasty breath of pestilence upon which one shall not look.

Dogma (1999)

When God talks, it's with gorgeously drowsy cadences and a British accent, courtesy of Alan Rickman as Metatron, voice of God. And when God appears, it's as Alanis Morissette. Oh, and sometimes God is just a nice little old man, who hangs out on the boardwalk at the Jersey Shore playing Skee-ball and handing out all the tickets he wins to little kids.

. . . continued

Oh, God *(1977)*

God appears as George Burns, complete with cigar, golf hat, Coke bottle glasses, endless supply of vaudeville jokes, and a willingness to admit to his mistakes, like avocados (made the pit too big—oh well, win some, lose some).

Monty Python and the Holy Grail *(1975)*

God is a cartoon cutout of a stern-faced, bearded man (actually, a famous nineteenth-century British cricket player!) who appears in the sky, encircled by clouds, to the tune of a celestial choir ahh-ahhh-ahhhhhing. However, the Lord has no patience for groveling or averting one's eyes—apparently such kowtowing gets really old after a few millennia.

Steambath *(1973)*

God appears as a Puerto Rican steam bath attendant (José Pérez) who rather enjoys hanging out with folks who have recently, er, kicked the bucket.

Mr. Destiny *(1990)*

God, played by Michael Caine, is a sympathetic bartender with just the right brew to give you self-insight, a newfound gratitude, and of course, no hangover.

Star Trek V *(1989)*

God is suspiciously *Wizard of Oz*–esque, with a baritone voice and the face of an old man that appears among roiling blue clouds and electrical storms on some faraway planet. But when "God" starts acting all Old Testament and zaps Kirk for doubting His identity, of course "God" is revealed to be just another alien life force with an agenda. Don't you just hate when that happens?

▪ *American Graffiti* (1973)

Stars: Richard Dreyfuss, Ronny Howard, Paul Le Mat, Charlie Martin Smith, Candy Clark, Cindy Williams, Harrison Ford, Mackenzie Phillips, Suzanne Somers, Wolfman Jack
Director: George Lucas
Writers: George Lucas, Gloria Katz, Willard Huyck

It's the last night before Curt (Richard Dreyfuss) and Steve (Ron Howard, barely out of his Opie years) are to leave for college out east, and Curt isn't sure he's ready to leave behind all that's familiar to him. Well, how can you blame him, when he lives in a hyper-stylized vision of youth culture of the 1950s, with big-finned Oldsmobiles cruising the strip, ten-cent Coca-Colas brought right to your car by a drive-in waitress on roller skates, and a soundtrack of the best of fifties' rock and roll, spun by DJ Wolfman Jack? Give Curt some Perry Como, a Dodge sedan, and a night spent eating meat loaf and ketchup in some prefab ranch house while watching *Gunsmoke* and maybe his sense of adventure would be a little more heightened.

As Curt vacillates about leaving for college, his sister, Laurie (Cindy Williams), is working reverse psychology on her boyfriend, Steve, to get him to stick with the status quo of their relationship. The local going-nowhere-fast Brylcreemed hotshot in a chopped thirties Ford, John (Paul Le Mat), is doing his best to avoid a drag race with a new cowboy in town (Harrison Ford), afraid that it's time for him to relinquish his title of fastest on the strip and retire into grease-monkey obscurity. And a tantalizing blonde (Suzanne Somers) in a white T-Bird keeps eluding Curt, forcing him to stop waiting for some gorgeous promise of perfection to sweep into his life and instead embrace his unknown future.

Reluctant to close one door and open another? Let *American Graffiti* remind you that indulging in nostalgia a little while longer can be harmless fun. But when the sun begins to rise, don't forget that there are even greater adventures ahead of you.

The superior man bends his attention to what is radical.

—Confucius

■ *This Is Spiñal Tap* (1984)

Stars: *Michael McKean, Harry Shearer, Christopher Guest, Rob Reiner, June Chadwick, Tony Hendra*

Director: *Rob Reiner*

Writers: *Christopher Guest, Michael McKean, Rob Reiner, Harry Shearer*

It can be difficult to let go of our dreams, particularly when we still recall the taste of the good life that came with success but is beginning to fade. Yet there comes a time when we all have to accept that in the bright daylight of a summer afternoon, our aspirations and our egos look awfully disproportionate to our reality . . . particularly when we've lost top billing to a puppet show at the Six Flags amusement park.

The fellows in the rock-and-roll band Spiñal Tap would like to believe they make cutting-edge progressive rock-and-roll records, but haven't quite got a handle on that fine line between clever and stupid. As they roll out for their American tour, their album *Sniff the Glove* is being ignored except by DJs who play it during their "What Ever Happened To?" segment, and their gigs are being canceled for lack of ticket sales.

David St. Hubbins (Michael McKean), Nigel Tufnel (Christopher Guest), and Derek Smalls (Harry Shearer) are dangerously close to total irrelevance, and the Stonehenge of their artistic aspirations is about to be trod upon by hired midgets in elf costumes. There are anxious meetings during which the boys circle the wagons and hurl accusations against their hapless manager (Tony Hendra), and frantic attempts to save face in front of their documentarian (Rob Reiner). There are hearty denials of their anxiety and fear, a quiet little war brewing over the well-meaning meddling of David's girlfriend (June Chadwick), and desperate attempts at beefing up their, uh, attributes for a rapidly dwindling audience.

Frankly, it will take more than well-placed prosthetic cucumbers to win back the glory that Spiñal Tap has lost. But as this movie shows, when you're able to get back to the heart of why you do what you do, and let go of your desire for the flash and glamour, you just might find that your new arena isn't such a disappointment after all.

The World According to Spiñal Tap

*Certainly, in the topsy-turvy world of
heavy rock, having a good solid piece
of wood in your hand is often useful.*
★ Tony Hendra as Spiñal Tap manager
Ian Faith in *This Is Spiñal Tap*

*I do not, for one, think that the prob-
lem was that the band was down.
I think that the problem may have been that there was a
Stonehenge monument on the stage that was in danger of
being crushed by a dwarf. All right? That tended to under-
state the hugeness of the object.*
★ Michael McKean as David St. Hubbins in *This Is Spiñal Tap*

It's such a fine line between stupid and clever.
★ Michael McKean as David St. Hubbins in *This Is Spiñal Tap*

*Well, I'm sure I'd feel much worse if I weren't under such
heavy sedation.*
★ Michael McKean as David St. Hubbins in *This Is Spiñal Tap*

*It's like fire and ice, basically. I feel my role in the band is to be
somewhere in the middle of that, kind of like luke-warm water.*
★ Harry Shearer as bassist Derek Smalls in *This Is Spiñal Tap*

. . . continued

Documentarian Marty DiBergi (Rob Reiner): Do you feel that
  playing rock-and-roll music keeps you a child? That is, keeps
  you in a state of arrested development?

Derek Smalls (Harry Shearer): No. No. No. I feel it's like, it's
  more like going, going to a, a national park or something.
  And there's, you know, they preserve the moose. And
  that's, that's my childhood up there onstage. That moose,
  you know.

Marty DiBergi: So when you're playing you feel like a preserved
  moose onstage?

Derek Smalls: Yeah.

★   from *This Is Spinal Tap*

■ *Les Misérables* (1998)
  Stars: Liam Neeson, Geoffrey Rush, Uma Thurman, Claire Danes
  Director: Bille August
  Writer: Rafael Yglesias, based on the novel by Victor Hugo

Eighteenth-century Frenchman Jean Valjean (Liam Neeson) feels he has an obligation to repay his higher power for a very lucky break, and we have to applaud his community investment development initiative—although the working conditions in the
factory he starts and his unfair labor practices regarding single mothers would definitely not qualify his stock for socially responsible investment funds. Really, all those
choleric complexions and purple under-eye circles make us wonder about the health-
care benefits.

Anyway, Valjean is even willing to make amends for these transgressions, adopting a young girl (Claire Danes) when her mother (Uma Thurman), a former employee of his, dies one of those whispering-through-cracked-lips deaths of consumption or some such. Unfortunately, Inspector Javert (Geoffrey Rush), a former nemesis of Valjean's, is tracking him across France, determined to make Valjean pay through the nose for stealing a loaf of bread decades ago. Will Valjean's example of atonement through action ever soften Javert's heart? Won't Javert ever let go of his vindictiveness about a crime that didn't even affect him, and get a life already?

When you're feeling guilty about a wrong you should've righted, check out this movie about making amends and moving on, and ask yourself whether it isn't time to let it go already.

I'd hoped Scott would look up to me, run the business of the family, head an evil empire just like his dear old dad, give him my love and the things I never had. Scott would think I was a cool guy, return the love I have, make me want to cry, be evil, but have my feelings too, change my life with Oprah and Maya Angelou. But Scott rejected me, c'est la vie, life is cruel, treats you unfairly, even so, a God there must be; Mini Me, you complete me.

★ Mike Myers as Dr. Evil in *Austin Powers: The Spy Who Shagged Me*

It Ain't Over 'Til It's Over

So you've been booted out of the prime advertising demographic and are into your relaxed-fit, farsighted years, and you're feeling that all that's left is bingo, buffet, and an inevitable slide into irrelevancy. Listen, even Springsteen and Dylan qualify for the AARP, so put an end to the pity party and have a little fun watching these movies about people who discovered that the sun wasn't setting on them quite as quickly as they'd thought.

Space Cowboys (2000)
Stars: *Clint Eastwood, Tommy Lee Jones, Donald Sutherland, Marcia Gay Harden, William Devane, James Garner*
Director: *Clint Eastwood*
Writers: *Ken Kaufman, Howard Klausner*

Just because we're not exactly cutting edge anymore doesn't mean that we're museum pieces. After all, a little wisdom born of age, a few long-forgotten tricks of the trade, and a humility earned after years of being considered outdated might be just what's needed to save all humankind from utter destruction and annihilation, right?

In this flick, four fellas who are in their egg-white-only-omelette and senior-discount years realize it's time to saddle up Old Paint and round up those lost dogies 'cause there just ain't nobody else who reads Skylab-era computer code. Still smarting because they never got their shot at traveling into space, these space cowboys smile weakly at the jokes that the newest generation of NASA scientists and engineers crack, and ready themselves for a mission to disable a satellite gone haywire. Hotdogger William "Hawk"

. . . *continued*

Hawkins (Tommy Lee Jones) can dust off his knowledge about landing without computer navigation systems, Frank Corvin (Clint Eastwood) can fix the programming, Tank Sullivan (James Garner) can act as chief engineer, and Jerry O'Neill (Donald Sutherland) can do his best to keep his dentures from floating away in zero gravity. Yes, despite the skepticism from the bigwigs at NASA, this "Team Daedalus" will prove that younger isn't necessarily better—and that just because your rear end is sagging asymmetrically doesn't mean you don't have the style and charm to woo lovers of all ages.

When you're feeling like the world wants to put you out to pasture just because you're on the wrong side of midlife, *Space Cowboys* is a fun reminder that obsolescence is in the eye of the beholder.

Pushing Hands (Tui shou) (1992)
Stars: Sihung Lung, Bo Z. Wang, Deb Snyder, Lai Wang,
     Haan Lee
Director: Ang Lee
Writer: Ang Lee, additional scenes by James Schamus

"Pushing Hands" is a Tai Chi Chuan technique that allows you to use your opponent's energy against himself, seemingly without effort, and quiet old Mr. Chu (Sihung Lung) mastered it as a tool of survival when swept up in the Cultural Revolution in Beijing. And now that he's just retired and moved in with his hell-on-wheels American daughter-in-law, boy, is he gonna need it.

Martha Chu (Deb Snyder) does have some excuses for her condescending and resentful attitude toward the non-English-speaking father-in-law who showed up on her doorstep last month. She's on a killer deadline for her much-anticipated first novel, she doesn't have a room of her own to work in,

. . . *continued*

and she's subsisting on salad and rice cakes, which not only doesn't balance yin and yang but would make anyone suffer hypoglycemic crankiness and brain fog.

Martha's husband, Alex (Bo Z. Wang), tries to find a balance between his spousal and filial duties, but it isn't long before the dignified and depressed senior Mr. Chu decides that he's got to have his independence. After all, if he can survive Mao's cultural genocide, he can survive a seven-hundred-dollar-a-month dishwasher's job in Chinatown. Then again, as a master of kung fu, he has extraordinary reserves of untapped power, so maybe there's an even better way to maintain his pride and autonomy, and live life on his own terms.

When you're feeling that life is pushing you around just because you're not the sprightly youngster you used to be, this movie will help you tap in to the inner dignity and strength that have been hidden inside you for too long and become the master of your own destiny.

Cocoon (1985)
Stars: Don Ameche, Wilford Brimley, Hume Cronyn, Brian Dennehy,
    Jack Gilford, Steve Guttenberg, Maureen Stapleton,
    Gwen Verdon, Jessica Tandy, Tahnee Welch
Director: Ron Howard
Writer: Tom Benedek, based on the novel by David Saperstein

Just what is the secret of eternal youth? Here's a movie that suggests that it's a refusal to give in to fear of the unknown, the courage to take a risk now and again, and a willingness to find common ground with those who are a little "different."

In this homey, feel-good Ron Howard movie, three elderly men from a retirement home discover that explorer Ponce de León wasn't so far off when he was looking for the fountain of youth in Florida. One day on a lark, the

. . . continued

fellas sneak into a neighbor's indoor swimming pool and emerge magically rejuvenated. Nearsighted Ben (Wilford Brimley) suddenly can read the last line on the eye chart at the DMV, Art (Don Ameche) can moon-walk and break-dance at the local disco, Joe (Hume Cronyn) discovers his cancer has gone into remission, and everybody gets laid for the first time since retirement. This improvement in the gentlemen's circulation and energy delights the ladies far more than shuffleboard and music therapy ever did, and puts a spring in everyone's step. When their secret gets out, however, the men find they have a more humanitarian use for their newfound vigor than just dancing the night away.

Feeling put out to pasture but don't have any friendly aliens in the vicinity to defy the laws of nature and gravity? Play a little hooky from what you think you're supposed to be doing and check out *Cocoon*. After all, it's reassuring to watch a group of folks who refuse to give in to fear and pessimism and are rewarded with a ticket to a never-ending adventure.

Chapter 10

All Together Now:
Love Is All Around You Movies

If the clouds are gathering on your emotional horizon, and it looks like one long and lonely stormy Monday up ahead, pop in one of these Love Is All Around You Movies and come in out of the rain. These films feature friends, families, and communities who band together when the sky is falling and learn how to provide shelter for each other and themselves through the power of love. They'll remind you that you can change the world just by changing your perspective, that you're never really alone as long as you are open to love in all its forms, and that when we join hands with each other, we can move mountains.

▪ *Forrest Gump* (1994)
Stars: Tom Hanks, Robin Wright Penn, Sally Field, Gary Sinise, Mykelti Williamson
Director: Robert Zemeckis
Writer: Eric Roth, based on the novel by Winston Groom

When life is leaving a bitter taste in your mouth, there's nothing like the movie that taught us all to think about life as a box of chocolates to remind you that the secret to happiness is learning how to enjoy any flavor in the assortment, even those gross fruity nougat ones.

On the surface of things, Forrest Gump (Tom Hanks) starts pulling fruity nougats out of the box at an early age. He is born with a very low IQ and needs braces on his legs in order to walk. But he's got his share of caramel centers as well—like a mom who loves him unconditionally (Sally Field), who teaches Forrest to look at his obstacles as opportunities, and to look at adversity, and even death, as just another part of life. This philosophy helps Forrest not only to survive, but to flourish. And although Forrest is a man who walks life's highway with braces on his legs, it's his ability to love and connect with every stranger that he meets that allows even a simpleton like Forrest to change the course of history. But then again, as Mama used to say, "Stupid is as stupid does."

Watch this movie when you're feeling stalled out on the road to happiness and let Forrest remind you that we never know how even the smallest moments in our lives can influence the course of global events, so it's best to approach each moment, and each person, with honesty and love, just in case.

 Forrest's Facts of Life

Mama always said, dying was a part of life.
    ★ Tom Hanks as Forrest Gump in *Forrest Gump*

My name's Forrest Gump. People call me Forrest Gump.
    ★ Tom Hanks as Forrest Gump in *Forrest Gump*

. . . *continued*

*I ran for three years, five months, and two days. When I was
hungry, I ate. When I was tired, I slept. When I had to go,
you know, I went!*

★　Tom Hanks as Forrest Gump in *Forrest Gump*

I'm not a smart man, but I know what love is.

★　Tom Hanks as Forrest Gump in *Forrest Gump*

▪ *The Englishman Who Went up a Hill but Came down a Mountain* (1995)
*Stars: Hugh Grant, Colm Meany, Ian McNeice, Ian Hart,
Tara Fitzgerald, Kenneth Griffith*
Director: Christopher Monger
Writer: Christopher Monger, from a story by Ivor Mongor

This is one of those delightful independent films about idiosyncratic folks in a pictur-
esque little village who set aside their differences, gather forces, learn to love thy neighbor,
and as a result create something that benefits and uplifts the entire community. And like
all the films in this genre, it makes you wish that you too had such strong bonds with the
people around you—and that you could just disappear for a few weeks amid rolling green
hills, whitewashed stone buildings, and charming pubs where time is irrelevant and everybody knows your name.

It is 1917 when two English surveyors, Reginald Anson (Hugh Grant) and George
Garrad (Ian McNeice), drive into a little Welsh village populated by odd characters like an
aging Bible-thumper, Reverend Jones (Kenneth Griffith), and a profiteering, womanizing
innkeeper named Morgan the Goat (Colm Meany). The plan is to measure the local
mountain so it can be included on the maps—Anson also nervously stutters something
about national security. Then the cartographers can move on to the next geographical
feature of note.

However, the beloved "mountain" may only be a mountain in the people's hearts and minds, for if it doesn't measure up to the standard thousand feet it won't be a mountain at all but a mere molehill. And as one might imagine, this doesn't go over well with a pub full of men with pints of bitters and nothing else to brag about but having the "first" mountain in Wales (at least, according to legend). These fellows transfer all their feelings of manhood and pride onto this big mound of dirt. Given that everyone in town is still wounded from the losses of so many of their men in trench warfare and the cruel coal mines, this isn't a matter of dispassionate scientific measurement or semantics, it's a matter of yet another inexplicable loss that's out of their control. Or is it?

If you're not quite convinced that faith can move mountains, or at least create them, watch this testament to the power of community determination and discover the healing power of a group labor of love.

Mountains, Not Molehills

All this fuss over what? Is it a hill, is it a mountain? Perhaps it wouldn't matter anywhere else, but this is Wales. The Egyptians built pyramids, the Greeks built temples, but we did none of that, because we had mountains. Yes, the Welsh were created by mountains: where the mountain starts, there starts Wales. If this isn't a mountain—well, if this isn't a mountain, then Anson might just as well redraw the border and put us all in England, God forbid.

★ Jack Walters as Grandfather in *The Englishman Who Went up a Hill but Came down a Mountain*

▪ *Alice's Restaurant* (1969)
   Stars: Arlo Guthrie, James Broderick, Patricia Quinn
   Director: Arthur Penn
   Writers: Venable Herndon, Arthur Penn, based on the Arlo Guthrie song
      "Alice's Restaurant Massacree," based on a real-life incident

Sometimes it seems that human nature ends up spoiling every utopian haven with bad vibes, jealousy, selfishness, and egos. Still, as this movie shows, if you can love with an open heart and reach out even to strangers, you can achieve grace and find yourself right where you're supposed to be, among friends.

It's 1965 and Arlo Guthrie—played by himself—doesn't know what he wants to do with his life, except to keep it, which means dodging the Vietnam War draft. When college and its deferment doesn't work out, he starts hanging out with some old friends, Ray (James Broderick) and Alice (Patricia Quinn), who have bought and refurbished an old church in small-town Massachusetts. Ray and Alice open their doors to all the wandering hippies—Alice finances the place by running a restaurant and Arlo helps out whenever he can, fronting his meager paycheck to some homeless kid or hauling garbage off to the dump. No good deed goes unpunished, however, and the result is an absurd charge of littering, which, in a bizarre twist, ends up determining whether or not Arlo will be packed off to Vietnam or able to spend his days carrying on his father's folksinging legacy. Meanwhile, Arlo just tries to savor the amazing grace he finds all around him, accept the love that's offered without ever taking advantage of kindly souls, and get down to the city regularly to visit his father, dying of Huntington's disease, to see if maybe he can make him smile again.

When you're feeling unloved and disconnected, and worn out by the demands of the modern world, this is the perfect movie tonic about the healing power of loving thy neighbor as thyself. Just remember to love thyself enough to put up the GONE SWIMMIN' sign once in a while, and have faith that someone else will serve up the soup of the day.

∽

The kingdom is within you and it is outside you.

—The Gospel of Thomas

∽

▪ *American Movie:* **The Making of Northwestern** (1999)
Stars: *Mark Borchardt, Mike Schank, Monica Borchardt, Bill Borchardt,*
Joan Petrie, Ken Keen, Tom Schimmels
Director: Chris Smith

There are those who might question the world's need for yet another low-budget, full-length black-and-white slasher film. So yes, it's a challenge not to giggle when one first watches mullet-headed, gawky Wisconsinite Mark Borchardt launch into an explanation of his artistic vision, inspired by *The Seventh Seal* and *Night of the Living Dead*, even as he's piling up his "Final Notice" bills. Frankly, even Borchardt's family thinks he's a world-class loser (he's thirty and still lives with his parents), although they're far too reserved to tell him outright. Instead, they indulge in passive-aggressive silences and mention to the documentarian that they personally think Mark is well suited for factory work.

And yet, while you might think that a documentary about a would-be filmmaker and high-school dropout who has to moonlight cleaning toilets in a graveyard for minimum wage would play as pathetic, somehow Borchardt's quixotic ambitions are oddly uplifting. It soon becomes clear that the products of his artistic expression may be, well, gross and obnoxious, and not exactly Bergman-esque. But they do capture the fear and anxiety of his working-class life. And while so many of his peers settle for soul-crushing day jobs and bury the pain of their broken dreams, Mark continually uses his pain as inspiration for his filmmaking.

Moreover, his passion for his project fuels almost everyone around him—his three children, his newly sober friends, and his admiring girlfriend—all of whom want to feel needed, important, and a part of something larger than themselves. They all pitch in and find comfort and even meaning in holding equipment, helping set up shots, and recording the requisite bloodcurdling screams. Even Mark's miserly grandfather, Bill Borchardt, who is accustomed to spending his days drinking far too much peppermint schnapps and sadly recalling the songs and poetry of his youth, rediscovers the joy of dreams and goals thanks to Mark.

Will Mark Borchardt ever achieve his American dream of a feature film and a decent-size house on a corner lot somewhere in southeast Wisconsin? Perhaps. Perhaps not. But if there's one thing this movie celebrates, it's the process of making art and the enriching camaraderie of those who lend their enthusiasm and hard work to that process. Watch it when you're feeling isolated and filled with regret, and see if it doesn't inspire you to gather your flock, pick a destination, and begin to fly again.

Them's Fightin' Words

What's your American dream? You can't stop now, man. What are you gonna do, sit outside of a trailer? We'll film you sittin' outside of a trailer, man. We ain't gonna live sittin' outside of a trailer.
★ Mark Borchardt to his grandfather, Bill Borchardt, in *American Movie: The Making of* Northwestern

Is that what you want to do with your life? Suck down peppermint schnapps and try to call Morocco at two in the morning?
★ Mark Borchardt in *American Movie: The Making of* Northwestern

Bev's Culinarytherapy: When-the-Chips-Are-Down Chocolate Chip Cookies MAKES 2 DOZEN

It's true you know, sometimes accidents really are happy. When Ruth Wakefield, owner of the Whitman Inn in Massachusetts, invented the chocolate chip cookie in 1930, she did so quite by accident. Ruth intended to whip up a batch of her famous butter drop cookies. Fortunately for all of us, destiny intervened, and a handful of chocolate chips tumbled into Ruth's mixing bowl, and the chocolate chip cookie was born. Here's one of my favorite variations on Ruth's main theme, which happened quite by accident, when I dropped a little chili powder into my mixing bowl. Now, whenever the chips are down, I make a plate big enough to comfort the whole neighborhood.

Here's what you'll need:

1 cup butter, softened
¾ cup granulated sugar
¾ cup brown sugar
2 eggs
2 teaspoons vanilla
1 teaspoon baking soda

2 cups all-purpose flour
1 teaspoon salt
Pinch chili powder
12 ounces milk chocolate chunks
6 ounces chopped macadamia nuts

Here's how you do it:

In a large mixing bowl, cream butter and sugar. Add eggs and vanilla and whip until the batter is light. Gradually add the dry ingredients and beat until smooth. Stir in the chocolate and nuts and whatever else happens to fall into the batter by accident. (Hey, it worked for Ruth.) Then fashion the dough into small balls, about the size of a Ping-Pong ball,

place on a greased cookie sheet, and bake at 375°F until the cookies are a light golden brown. Then open the door and invite the neighbors in.

■ **Blow Dry** *(2001)*
Stars: Natasha Richardson, Alan Rickman, Rachel Griffiths, Josh Hartnett
Director: Paddy Breathnach
Writer: Simon Beaufoy

When the annual British hairdressing competition comes to the small town of Keighly, a family full of split ends and a community long since grown limp and lifeless suddenly find a common thread and tease and comb their way to redemption, supported by the hidden underpinnings of love.

Tonsorial sensations Shelley (Natasha Richardson) and Phil Allan (Alan Rickman), formerly husband and wife, haven't spoken since Shelley ran off with the female hair model just before the big show ten years previous. They share a son, Brian (Josh Hartnett), a best friend, Sandra (Rachel Griffiths), as well as a talent for hair and a deep love for each other. They also, however, share a deeply layered history complete with some pretty chunky highlights that just didn't manage to grow out that well. And so they remain at odds, until the hair show comes round one more time, and Shelley, recently diagnosed with breast cancer, tries to take the old act out on the road for one final encore. The camaraderie of competition, the joy of working together once more, as well as the idea of losing Shelley, makes every member of the team realize how much they need and love each other. And as they pick up the strands of their tangled braid and reweave their family bond, they draw the entire community into the exuberant creativity of their coiffure of love.

Can't We All Just Get Along?

*You know, rather than get confrontational, why
don't we all just sit down together, have some
salad with dolphin-safe tuna, and see if we can't start a dialogue?*

★ Brendan Fraser as the sensitive Elliot in *Bedazzled*

*Reg (John Cleese): All right, but apart from the sanitation, medicine,
education, wine, public order, irrigation, roads, the fresh water
system, and public health, what have the Romans ever done for us?*
Attendee: Brought peace?
Reg: Oh, peace—shut up!

★ from *Monty Python's Life of Brian*

■ *Black Like Me* (1964)
Star: James Whitmore
Director: Carl Lerner
Writers: Carl Lerner, Gerda Lerner, based on the memoir of John Howard Griffin

In the midst of ignorance, disrespect, and downright hatred, it's amazing how even the smallest acts of human kindness from our fellow man can water the seeds of hope. This movie, based on a true story of a white Texan journalist (John Howard Griffin) who dyed his skin and hair dark in order to pass as a black man as he traveled through the South, certainly proves that decency and compassion can survive even amid soul-crushing ignoramuses.

The first time we see John Finley Horton (James Whitmore), he looks like he's just a white guy in blackface. But in the Deep South in the early 1960s, anyone with dark skin was immediately deemed a Negro, so he's expected to sit in the back of the bus and add "Yessir" to the end of every sentence. To whites, Horton is an object of scorn and contempt. They think his life's purpose is to kowtow to and serve them—oh, and amuse them with stories of his prurient behavior. Of course, he doesn't actually *have* any stories of prurient behavior, but that doesn't stop them from leaning over with a you-can-tell-me leer and asking him. Meanwhile, to blacks, Horton is a trustworthy man until proven otherwise, and a fellow who needs to be pulled aside and taught the rules of the road before he becomes walking bait for local rednecks.

Even as Horton struggles to handle the rage that's building up inside him, the endless assault of insults, and his dwindling sense of who he really is, he comes to realize that when you least expect it, some fella will offer you an extra doughnut, a free room, and a genuine smile of friendship that will help you to carry on another day.

So when you find yourself disgusted by the worst of human nature, check out *Black Like Me* and be reassured that even when cruelty seems to dominate, the seedlings of human decency have a way of taking a foothold in the garden.

Reel to Real

John Howard Griffin was a World War II vet who worked as a medic for the French Resistance. He was blinded by the war and did not regain his sight for twelve years, which may have kept him from seeing what people looked like but didn't prevent him from seeing how they are.

One family on earth are we/Throughout its widest span/O help us everywhere to see/The brotherhood of man.
—from the hymn "Our Father, Our Dear Name Doth Show"

■ *The Year of Living Dangerously* (1982)

Stars: *Mel Gibson, Sigourney Weaver, Linda Hunt*
Director: *Peter Weir*
Writers: *C. J. Koch, Peter Weir, based on the novel by C. J. Koch*

It is often said that if you want to know the world, love others. And such is the case with fledgling Aussie reporter Guy Hamilton (Mel Gibson), who goes to Jakarta in 1965 seeking his Pulitzer prize–winning story during the final year of Sukarno's Communist regime.

Guy is a man without a country or a community of any kind in this strange town. The doors of the local culture are shut to him. And even the old-boys' network of English reporters, who treat this capital of the developing world like an English gentlemen's club, don't seem too interested in him. But there is a compassion and a vulnerability in Guy, and not just because of those azure-as-an-Aspen-sky-in-September eyes either, that appeals to Billy Kwan (Linda Hunt). Billy, a diminutive but fiery native photojournalist who feels deeply for the plight of his people, chooses Guy to tell the truth about the suffering in Jakarta, and this man without a country suddenly finds himself the mouthpiece of a developing nation.

Billy leads Guy on a personally guided tour through the highs and lows of Indonesian culture, knitting a web of understanding and compassion between the Western world and the developing world, and in some small way healing both cultures through the love and understanding that is forged when two such differing cultures join hands under the curse of interesting times.

&

But I always think that the best way to know God is to love many things.

—Vincent van Gogh

Do You Believe in Magic?

In movieland, the more hardened the skeptic, the more likely he or she is to smack straight up against the unexplainable. Is some mystical force at play, or just a bunch of really talented special-effects guys? In these movies, magic really does happen when people open their hearts and minds to the love that is around them, and to the mystery in the universe. Watch them when you need an infusion of faith that miracles really do happen.

FairyTale: A True Story (1997)
Stars: Peter O'Toole, Harvey Keitel, Florence Hoath, Elizabeth Earl,
    Phoebe Nicholls, Paul McGann
Director: Charles Sturridge
Writer: Ernie Contreras, based on a story by Albert Ash,
    Tom McLoughlin, Ernie Contreras

The beautiful countryside of England is rapidly changing from green to black as the soot of the Industrial Revolution settles upon hill and dale, and the forces of progress, world war, and twentieth-century rationalism are rendering spiritualists and theosophical societies obsolete. Yes, it's time to put aside silly folk notions and focus on what's really important—like modernizing the mill so that twelve-year-olds can stop wasting time in school and play and get to work feeding the capitalist machine.

But then, two little cousins—Francie (Elizabeth Earl) and Elsie (Florence Hoath)—are discovered to have taken photographs of fairies down by the creek. The images are so convincing that their mother and aunt, Polly (Phoebe Nicholls), who has been distraught ever since her son died, suddenly begins to believe again in the world of spirits and sprites. And while this is

. . . continued

not the age of e-mail attachments and digital cameras, there are aggressive newspaper reporters roaming about, and before long all of England is debating whether there are fairies in Bradford, and whether adults or only children can see them. In a country where the names of mythical knights and their fair ladies are now bestowed on dogs, the thought that the fairies haven't deserted the people who've abandoned the land catches the imagination of all. Will the venerable Sir Arthur Conan Doyle (Peter O'Toole) and master illusionist Harry Houdini (Harvey Keitel) discover the truth about the girls and the fairies? And does anyone really want them to?

This enchanting little movie, based on a true story, will have you fondly remembering the days when you accepted magic unquestioningly. Watch it when you're feeling bruised by the modern world and want to recapture the wonderment of childhood.

Out of the Mouths of Babes

Grown-ups don't know how to believe.
★ Elizabeth Earl as Francie Griffiths in
FairyTale: A True Story

*Reverend Russell (David Strathairn): What are
you doing sitting in a corner, Simon?
Simon Birch (Ian Michael Smith): Thinking
about God.
Reverend Russell: In a corner?
Simon: Faith is not in a floor plan.*
★ from *Simon Birch*

. . . continued

The Third Miracle (1999)

Stars: Ed Harris, Anne Heche, Armin Mueller-Stahl, Charles Haid,
   Michael Rispoli, Barbara Sukowa
Director: Agnieszka Holland
Writers: John Romano, Richard Vetere, based on the novel by Richard Vetere

Father Frank (Ed Harris), an investigator of mystical events, knows all the tricks. For instance, if you need to bring pilgrims to your parish, paint a statue's eyes with pig fat and it will "bleed" tears. No wonder Frank is called the miracle killer, and no one's exactly jumping up to embrace him when he shows up at a little Polish parish that has its very own virgin statue that weeps in the November rain. But then it turns out that Frank has a second chance at proving a miracle after all. And having been burned before when he investigated what turned out to be a bogus one, he's struggling to decide whether that's a good thing or a bad thing. Meanwhile, Roxanne (Anne Heche), the free-spirited daughter of the humble Catholic layperson who is being considered for beatification, is appalled by Father Frank's investigation. She thinks her mother, Helen (Barbara Sukowa), was less a saint than a do-gooder who needed to spend a little more time tending to her own child.

Despite their different worldviews, the legacy of Helen—who may very well be responsible for not one, not two, but maybe even three miracles—forces Roxanne and Frank to struggle together to put aside their pain so that they can see the truth, even if that truth threatens to turn their world on its ear.

If you've been feeling unsettled about what you believe and what you want to believe, pop in *The Third Miracle* and enjoy having the security of logic, science, and mystery all at the same time.

. . . continued

Dragonfly (2002)
Stars: *Kevin Costner, Susanna Thompson, Kathy Bates*
Director: *Tom Shadyac*
Writers: *David Seltzer, Brandon Camp, Mike Thompson,*
　　based on a story by Brandon Camp and Mike Thompson

Dr. Joe Darrow (Kevin Costner), whose wife recently disappeared in Venezuela, is a hyperrational doctor who's quite certain that his beloved is gone forever and that death is the closing of a door. He believes there's a perfectly logical explanation for mysterious midnight tappings at the window, paperweights jumping off nightstands by themselves, and child cancer patients who have flat-lined and come back knowing your name and all sorts of weird details about you. It's just, it'd be nice if someone could actually provide these explanations so Joe could stop thinking about the lack of resolution to his wife, Emily's, death—after all, her body was never found after that terrible accident. Frankly, he'd just like to go on being irritable and dumbfounded and live in his big empty house with his overwhelming grief until time allows it to dissipate. But then those sweet little patients on the cancer ward, whom his late wife the oncologist made him promise to visit in her absence, keep saying and doing mysterious things.

Darrow's neighbor (Kathy Bates) suggests a long-overdue vacation, but wouldn't you know that ends up just giving him more clues from beyond? Now he's just got to go adventuring into the unknown to reclaim something that's been lost. Can't a man get any peace around here without all this "Crossing Over" stuff floating into his consciousness at every turn?

Now, you may find the edge-of-your-seat mystery in *Dragonfly* a bit overindulgent in the end. We could've done with a one- or two-hankie denouement instead of an all-out waterfall effect, and that ridiculous special-

. . . continued

effects/action-adventure sequence is an annoyingly unnecessary distraction. But if you've ever been guided by signs that sound preposterous when you try to explain them to someone else in the light of day, this movie will definitely reassure you that mysterious road maps can direct you to exactly where you want to go.

Words are but nests, the meanings are the birds,
Body the bed through which the spirit-river flows.

—Rumi

■ *Billy Elliot* (2000)
Stars: Jamie Bell, Gary Lewis, Jamie Draven, Julie Walters
Director: Stephen Daldry
Writer: Lee Hall

It's 1984, and the little town of Durham in North England is filled with tension between the coal miners, who are striking for a decent wage, and those who've seen the future of the working class under the Thatcher administration and are taking whatever wages they can get. And in Billy Elliot's home, his father (Gary Lewis) and brother (Jamie Draven) are growing more bitter each day as they face an increasingly dark future. The only escape from this sorry little town seems to be death or madness, until one day when the local dance teacher, Mrs. Wilkinson (Julie Walters), sees the spark of talent in Billy (Jamie Bell), a boy who would rather practice pliés than his left hook. So Billy secretly ditches boxing class and starts being tutored by Mrs. Wilkinson. Inspired by his late mother's last letter to him, in which she urged her son to always be himself, Billy stands up to the contempt and rage of his family. And to the tunes of T. Rex, he manages to jig his way into their good graces.

Even more amazingly, Billy shows this tough community of coal miners the future . . . and it is wearing a tutu. Suddenly, everyone is scraping together what little money he has to send Billy to London for a dance audition. Billy becomes a living symbol of the hope of change and renewal for all of them.

When you're feeling pessimistic about the future and need an inspiring reminder of how all of us are raised up when we pull together and support the talents of the young people around us, watch *Billy Elliot*, and feel your heart soar like a swan in flight.

 ## Words to Live By

I don't want champagne. I am champagne.
★ Samuel L. Jackson as Doyle Gipson
in *Changing Lanes*

This is an occasion for genuinely tiny knickers.
★ Renée Zellweger as Bridget Jones in *Bridget Jones's Diary*

▪ *Edward Scissorhands* (1990)
Stars: Johnny Depp, Winona Ryder, Dianne Wiest
Director: Tim Burton
Writer: Caroline Thompson, based on a story by Tim Burton and Caroline Thompson

Edward (Johnny Depp) is a really handsome, androgynous, and distinctly goth-inspired neo-Frankenstein who is unable to share love because he was created with scissors in place of hands. Therefore it just stands to reason that he will eviscerate anyone he embraces, which can make it pretty hard to lend a hand at community functions, or shake hands and greet new friends. So Edward resigns himself to living alone, in an abandoned castle on the top of a lonely hill, unremarked by anyone, until Avon calls.

When Peg Boggs (Dianne Wiest), a quirky Avon lady from the stylized suburbs of Tim Burton's imagination, gets a look at Edward, she immediately feels compassion for him and brings Edward home to live with her hypersuburban family, in their hypersuburban house. The only trouble is her hypersuburban neighbors are a tad aghast at the harbinger of the Marilyn Manson years living in the Boggs's guest room. And Peg's daughter, Kim (Winona Ryder), isn't too happy about sharing her home with a human Ginsu. But when Edward and his new family and community find a way to turn Edward's blades into accolades, their collective creativity and love for each other change the face of the whole neighborhood.

If you've been feeling like a square peg in a round hole, let *Edward Scissorhands* remind you that when you accept who you are, capitalize on your strengths, and surround yourself with people who appreciate your unique gifts, then you can make a world of difference, just by being yourself.

Dianne's Delectables

I'm still a star! I never play frumps or virgins.
★ Dianne Wiest as Helen Sinclair in *Bullets over Broadway*

Helen (Dianne Wiest): My ex-husband used to say, "If you're gonna go down, go down with the best of them!"
Sid Loomis (Harvey Fierstein): Which ex-husband?
Helen: Oh, I don't know which ex-husband. The one with the mustache.
★ Dianne Wiest as Helen Sinclair in *Bullets over Broadway*

■ *The Human Comedy* (1943)

Stars: Mickey Rooney, Frank Morgan, Van Johnson, Fay Bainter, Donna Reed
Director: Clarence Brown
Writer: Howard Estabrook, based on a story by William Saroyan

Sometimes it's nice to curl up with one of those unapologetically sentimental World War II–era classics and escape to a world where people always speak in a loving manner, pray simply and eloquently when they are afraid, and seem to exist in a perpetual state of grace. But be forewarned: You'll either let forth a waterfall of tears when you watch this one or roll your eyes at its wholesomeness.

Many of the residents of Ithaca, California, know that music brings comfort to the poor of spirit: The Macauley girls and their mother play the harp and harmonize their soprano voices to ease the pain of losing their father. Their brother (Van Johnson) plays "Danny Boy" on the concertina to his army buddies as they wait for orders to ship out, knowing that many of them won't return. And when middle son Homer (Mickey Rooney), a telegram messenger, is aching over having to inform a Mexican American mother that her only son has died in action, peace begins to blanket him as he listens to the mother's plaintive voice singing an old folk song from her homeland.

Now, you know that with a main character off at war, and a related character who's the town's bearer of all those "The War Department regrets to inform you" telegrams, it's only a matter of time before there's a crescendo of sorrow and redemption, and a heartwarming message about being grateful for the people we love and the people we had a chance to know before they departed. And yet, this movie also reminds us to celebrate the people we have just met, who will inevitably enter our lives when we are experiencing a void.

When you're feeling like a lone melody, why not try *The Human Comedy*? You just may begin to hear the sweet voices surrounding you.

Can I Get an "Amen"?

Prayer is only another name for good, clean, direct thinking. When you pray, think. Think well what you're saying. Make your thoughts into things that are solid and that way your prayer will have strength, and that strength will become a part of you: body, mind, and spirit.

★ Walter Pidgeon as Mr. Gruffydd the preacher in *How Green Was My Valley*

That's not why I pray, Harry. I pray because I can't help myself. I pray because I'm helpless. I pray because the need flows out of me all the time, waking and sleeping. It doesn't change God, it changes me. ★ Anthony Hopkins as C. S. Lewis in *Shadowlands*

I have issues with anyone who treats faith as a burden instead of a blessing. You people don't celebrate your faith; you mourn it.

★ Salma Hayek as Serendipity in *Dogma*

Nancy's Momentous Minutiae: It's Just a Movie, Guys . . . Or Is It?

Nazis, not yet in power in Germany when the 1930 anti-war film *All Quiet on the Western Front* was released, nevertheless protested it by releasing rats into movie theaters where it was playing and shouting Nazi slogans at the screen.

Washington insiders groused that *Mr. Smith Goes to Washington* (1939) portrayed them in a bad light, but at the same time several fascist countries banned the film because they felt it was a feature-length advertisement for the virtues of democracy.

■ *And the Band Played On* (1993)
   Stars: *Matthew Modine, Alan Alda, Lily Tomlin, Richard Gere,*
      Anjelica Huston
   Director: *Roger Spottiswoode*
   Writer: *Arnold Shulman, based on the book by Randy Shilts*

Randy Shilts's dramatized account of the discovery of the AIDS virus, and of the Reagan administration's apathy in the face of a growing epidemic, is one of the most disturbing but inspiring stories about the difference that a group of people can make when they commit themselves to a common cause. This movie reminds us all that where there's a will, there's a way, and when we feel compassion for each other, and reach out to one another, we can move mountains, even in the Reagan eighties.

Matthew Modine stars as Dr. Don Francis, a field director with the Centers for Disease Control charged with investigating emergent epidemics worldwide. When GRID (Gay Related Immune Deficiency) or the "gay cancer" first emerges in San Francisco, Dr. Francis is sent to investigate and winds up in a ground war against the powers that be in Washington, who refuse to acknowledge that people are dying.

At Dr. Francis's side in this first battle of the war on AIDS is a band of passionate and dedicated health-care professionals (including Lily Tomlin as the fiery health department inspector Dr. Selma Dritz, who is charged with shutting down the bathhouses), as well as the gay and lesbian community at large, who band together to meet a mighty foe because all they have is each other. Against them in the battle are ignorance, fear, lack of funding, and an administration that went for eight years during the height of the epidemic without ever once mentioning the word *AIDS*.

This is a great movie to watch when you're feeling powerless and need to rekindle your fire. Let the doctors and health-care workers, and the gay men and women of San Francisco who loved each other enough to change the world, inspire you to act up wherever you see injustice in your corner of the world, because where there is no justice, there is no peace.

This may be the first epidemic in history of which no one officially died.

★ Matthew Modine as Dr. Don Francis in *And the Band Played On*

■ *The Grapes of Wrath* (1940)
Stars: Henry Fonda, Jane Darwell, John Carradine
Director: John Ford
Writer: Nunnally Johnson, based on the novel by John Steinbeck

When troubles are piling up and the promised land lies miles away across a desert of despair, it's empowering to be reminded that you're not the only one on the highway—and that even the most impoverished and frightened among us can find the courage to trust and help each other.

After fifty years of farming on the same lot in Oklahoma, the Joad family is being driven out by the Dust Bowl—with the help of the bank and the management company, and a big old bulldozer that crunches their house into kindling.

Tom Joad (Henry Fonda), along with Casy (John Carradine), the local preacher who has lost his faith, a neighbor or two, and all the Joads including Grandma and Grandpa, pack everything they can into an old Ford truck and head out to sunny California, lured by handbills promising plenty of jobs at good wages. Too bad they didn't bring a radio, or they might've learned that about ten thousand other families have the same idea. Yes, there's barely enough food to go around in the makeshift camps, wages are dropping so low you couldn't feed a man on a day's pay—much less a family—and anyone who even whispers the word *union* seems to suddenly disappear, never to be seen again.

With all these migrants descending upon their area, many of the locals in the Golden State are fearful for their own livelihood. Clearly, the only power the migrants have is in numbers, but can they find the courage to band together, ignore the rumbling in their bellies, and face the nightsticks wielded by corrupt cops? Or will they give in to panic?

Will Casy find a new faith? And can Tom keep a lid on the anger that's boiling up inside of him?

When your supply of courage is running low, check out *The Grapes of Wrath* and be reminded of the survival power of people who replace fear with love, pull together, and retain their humanity, drawing strength from the small acts of human kindness that exist even when the darkest storms blow through the land.

We Shall Overcome

*I wouldn't pray just for an old man that's dead,
    'cause he's all right. If I was to pray, I'd pray
for folks that's alive and don't know which way to turn.*

★ John Carradine as Casy in *The Grapes of Wrath*

*We keep a comin'. We're the people that live. They can't wipe us
out, and they can't lick us. We'll go on forever, Pa, 'cause we're
the people.*

★ Jane Darwell as Ma Joad in *The Grapes of Wrath*

*Maybe it's like Casy says—a fella ain't got a soul of his own, just a
little piece of a big soul, the one big soul that belongs to everybody.
Then . . . it don't matter. I'll be all around in the dark. I'll be
everywhere, wherever you can look. Wherever there's a fight
so hungry people can eat, I'll be there. Wherever there's a cop
beatin' up a guy, I'll be there. I'll be in the way guys yell when
they're mad. I'll be in the way kids laugh when they're hungry
and they know supper's ready. And when the people are eatin' the
stuff they raise and livin' in the houses they built, I'll be there too.*

★ Henry Fonda as Tom Joad in *The Grapes of Wrath*

Words to Live By

The day will come when, after harnessing space, the winds, the tides, and gravitation, we shall harness for God the energies of love. And on that day, for the second time in the history of the world, we shall have discovered fire.

★ Pierre Teilhard de Chardin

Index

A

Abagnale, Frank, Jr., 6
About a Boy, 56
About Schmidt, 79–80
Abrahams, Jim, 12
Accepting Personal
  Responsibility Movies,
  54–71
Ackroyd, Dan, 14
Adams, Joey Lauren, 157, 158
Adamson, Joy, 110
Adaptation, 75, 77
Addy, Mark, 10
*Adventures of Buckaroo Banzai
  Across the 8th Dimension, The*,
  74
Adventures of Ford Fairlane, The,
  153
Affair to Remember, An, 39
Affleck, Ben, 68, 93
Agony and the Ecstasy, The,
  49–50
Alda, Alan, 202
Alexander, Jane, 73, 122

Alford, Phillip, 78
Alice, 168–169
Alice's Restaurant, 185
All Quiet on the Western Front, 62,
  201
All That Heaven Allows, 81
All That Jazz, 21
All the President's Men,
  122–123
Allen, Jay Presson, 133
Allen, Penny, 97
Allen, Tim, 161
Allen, Woody, 168
Allgood, Sara, 32
Altered States, 67
Altman, Robert, 136
Ambrose, Lauren, 18
Ameche, Don, 24, 179, 180
Amélie, 43
Amenábar, Alejandro, 55
American Graffiti, 172
*American Movie: The Making of
  Northwestern*, 186–187
American Rhapsody, An, 96
Anatomy of a Murder, 62
And the Band Played On,
  202–203

Anders, Allison, 2
Anderson, Carl, 124
Anderson, James, 78
Angel Heart, 88
Aniston, Jennifer, 166
Annaud, Jean-Jacques, 117
Antianxiety Movies, 72–97
Antwone Fisher, 28
Apocalypse Now, 65, 66
Arachnophobia, 118
Arcand, Denys, 126
Arlen, Alice, 139
Armstrong, Gillian, 138
Armstrong, William H., 25
Ash, Albert, 193
Ashby, Hal, 52
Astaire, Fred, 13
August, Bille, 175
Austin, Michael, 112
*Austin Powers: The Spy Who
  Shagged Me*, 176
Austin Powers in Goldmember,
  127
Axton, Hoyt, 40
Ayres, Lew, 62
Azaria, Hank, 11, 153,
  154

B

Babenco, Hector, 50
Back to the Future, 62
Bacon, Kevin, 64
Badham, Mary, 78
Bailey, Fenton, 7
Bainter, Fay, 200
Bakker, Tammy Faye, 7, 8
Baldwin, Alec, 168, 169
Ball, Alan, 18
Ball, Lucille, 13
Ballard, Carroll, 40, 119
Balsam, Martin, 144
Bancroft, Anne, 132
Banger Sisters, The, 45
Barbato, Randy, 7
Bardot, Brigitte, 41
Barron, Robert V., 24
Barry, Raymond J., 162
Barrymore, Drew, 41
Bates, Kathy, 79, 102, 196
Batman Forever, 148
Battle for the Planet of the Apes, 115
Baum, L. Frank, 33
Baye, Nathalie, 67
Bayley, John, 36
Beaches, 44, 46
Beaufoy, Simon, 10, 189
Beautiful, 157–158
Bedazzled (1967), 88
Bedazzled (2000), 39, 89, 190
Beetlejuice, 84
Begley, Ed, 144
Begley, Louis, 79
Bell, Jamie, 197

Beneath the Planet of the Apes, 114
Benedek, Tom, 179
Bentley, James, 55
Bergman, Ingrid, 156
Bernstein, Carl, 122–123
Bernstein, Jon, 157
Bertolini, Christopher, 64
Best Little Whorehouse in Texas, The, 140, 149
Big Business, 46
Bill and Ted's Bogus Journey, 21, 87
Bill and Ted's Excellent Adventure, 24
Billy Elliot, 197–198
Black Like Me, 190–191
Black Stallion, The, 40
Blackboard Jungle, 130, 131
Blanchett, Cate, 2, 47, 138
Blasi, Vera, 163
Blethyn, Brenda, 4, 5, 156
Blow Dry, 189
Bluteau, Lothaire, 126
Bochner, Hart, 132
Bolger, Ray, 33
Bontrager, Velda, 8
Borchardt, Bill, 186, 187
Borchardt, Mark, 186–187
Borchardt, Monica, 186
Born Free, 110–111
Born on the Fourth of July, 162
Bowling for Columbine, 121–122
Bracco, Lorraine, 70
Braga, Sonia, 50
Bragg, Melvyn, 124
Branagh, Kenneth, 30, 31, 104, 105
Brando, Marlon, 65, 66

Breakfast at Tiffany's, 79, 153
Breathnach, Paddy, 189
Bridges, Jeff, 57
Bridget Jones's Diary, 198
Brimley, Wilford, 20, 179, 180
Bring Out Your Inner Glow Goop (Bev's Culinarytherapy), 4
Broadbent, Jim, 12, 36, 137
Brock, Jeremy, 138
Broderick, James, 97, 185
Brody, Adrien, 26
Brooks, Albert, 85, 86
Brooks, Kristen, 100
Brooks, Nate, 100
Brooks, Richard, 130
Brosnan, Pierce, 19
Brown, Clarence, 200
Brown, Harry, 60
Broyles, William, Jr., 104
Bryant, Joy, 28
Bullets Over Broadway, 199
Burden, Bob, 153
Burke, Billie, 33
Burns, George, 171
Burroughs, Edgar Rice, 112
Burton, Tim, 198
Buscemi, Steve, 76, 77, 149
Byrne, Gabriel, 89

C

Cage, Nicolas, 75, 77
Caine, Michael, 4, 5, 92, 127, 171

Cameron, James, 102
Camp, Brandon, 196
Capote, Truman, 79
Capra, Frank, 115
Cardoso, Patricia, 158
Cargol, Jean-Pierre, 123
Carlyle, Robert, 10
Carradine, John, 203, 204
Carrere, Tia, 132, 133
Carter, Helena Bonham, 104, 115
Cartwright, Jim, 4
Casino, 71
Cast Away, 104
Catch Me If You Can, 67–68
Cattaneo, Peter, 10
Cazale, John, 97
Chabrol, Claude, 55
Chadwick, June, 173
Changing Lanes, 93–94, 198
Chaplin, Charlie, 27
Charlotte Gray, 138
Chase, Chevy, 39
Chase, David, 70
Cher, 139
Chermayeff, Maro, 100
Chicago, 39, 146, 147
Cilento, Diane, 49
Clark, Candy, 172
Clark, Dick, 121
Clark, Matt, 20
Clarkson, Patricia, 110
Cleese, John, 104, 105, 190
Clift, Montgomery, 23, 60
Clune, Adrienne, 100
Clune, Gordon, 100
Cobb, Lee J., 144
Cocoanuts, 13

Cocoon, 24, 179–180
Cohen, Joel, 161
Cohen, Jon, 58
Cole, Lester, 110
Coleman, Dabney, 139
Colgan, Eileen, 107–108
Colman, Ronald, 12, 115
Columbus, Chris, 6
Come On Up, We're Rising Movies, 16–34
Condon, Bill, 146
Conquest of the Planet of the Apes, 114
Conrad, Joseph, 65
Conroy, Frances, 18
Conselman, William M., 141
Constantine, Michael, 36
Contreras, Ernie, 193
Cooper, Chris, 75
Cooper, Gary, 22
Coppola, Francis Ford, 65
Corbett, John, 36, 37
Corduner, Allan, 137
Corr, Eugene, 119
Cort, Bud, 52
Costner, Kevin, 196
Country, 20
Courtney, Jeni, 107
Cousins, Christian, 128
Cousins, Joseph, 128
Cox, Brian, 62, 63, 73
Cox, Paul, 137
Crawford, Joan, 155, 156
Crichton, Michael, 102
Crisp, Donald, 32
Cromwell, James, 64
Cronyn, Hume, 179, 180
Crossroads, 14–15

Crothers, Scatman, 109
Crudup, Billy, 138
Cruise, Tom, 58, 64, 65, 162
Crystal, Billy, 87
Cukor, George, 155
Cumming, Alan, 44
Cuthbert, Neil, 153

Dafoe, Willem, 126, 162
Daldry, Stephen, 197
Damon, Matt, 68, 69
Danes, Claire, 175, 176
Dangerfield, Rodney, 89
Daniels, Jeff, 118
Darabont, Frank, 104
Dart, Iris Rainer, 44
Darwell, Jane, 203, 204
Davie, Gordon, 51
Davis, Bette, 69
Davis, Hope, 79, 80
Davis, Tamra, 14
Day, Doris, 41
Days of Thunder, 148
De Bont, Jan, 102
De Croisset, Francis, 155
De Niro, Robert, 71, 88, 104, 105
De Wolf, Nat, 152
Death to Smoochy, 142–143
Deconstructing Harry, 87–88
Deep Impact, 101, 103
Defending Your Life, 85–86
DeMille, Nelson, 64

Demme, Jonathan, 22, 51
Dench, Judi, 36
Dennehy, Brian, 119, 179
Depp, Johnny, 198
Deutsch, Helen, 149
Devane, William, 177
Devil's Advocate, 90
Devil's Playground, 8–9
Devine, Loretta, 59
DeVito, Danny, 12, 142
Diaries of Vaslav Nijinsky, The, 137
DiCaprio, Leonardo, 67, 91, 102, 103
DiCillo, Tom, 76
Dick, Philip K., 58
Dillon, Matt, 2, 147
Dinklage, Peter, 77
Divine Secrets of the Ya-Ya Sisterhood, 10
Docter, Peter, 161
Dog Day Afternoon, 97
Dogma, 170, 201
Dolman, Bob, 45
Donan, Stanley, 88
Donoghue, Mary Agnes, 44
Dorfman, David, 73
Douglas, Illeana, 2, 147
Douglas, Melvyn, 155
Dr. Strangelove, 103
Dragonfly, 196–197
Draven, Jamie, 197
Dreisler, Theodore, 60
Dreyfuss, Richard, 132, 172
Driver, Minnie, 157, 158
Dubus, André, 61
Duck Soup, 27
Duffy, Dave, 107

Duke, Patty, 149, 150
Dunne, Griffin, 152
Dunne, Philip, 32, 49
Dürrenmatt, Friedrich, 110
Duvall, Robert, 65, 66, 78, 101
Duvall, Shelley, 109

Earl, Elizabeth, 193
Eastwood, Clint, 177, 178
Ebb, Fred, 146
Eckhart, Aaron, 140
Edward Scissorhands, 198–199
Eisenberg, Hallie Kate, 157, 158
Eisenberg, Larry, 83
Elder, Lonne, III, 25
Elizabeth, 47–48
Elizondo, Hector, 163
Elliman, Yvonne, 124
Elwes, Cary, 102
Emerson, Ralph Waldo, 83
Emshwiller, Susan, 136
End of Days, 89–90
Engel, Samuel G., 141
Englishman Who Went up a Hill But Came down a Mountain, The, 5, 183–184
Ephron, Delia, 38
Ephron, Nora, 38, 139
Epperson, Tom, 2
Erin Brockovich, 140
Escape from the Planet of the Apes, 114

Estabrook, Howard, 200
Eyes of Tammy Faye, The, 7, 8
Eyre, Richard, 36

FairyTale: A True Story, 193–194
Falco, Edie, 70
Fanning, Dakota, 59
Fantastic Voyage, 3
Far From Heaven, 81–82
Farley, Walter, 40
Farrow, Mia, 168
Father of the Bride, 74
Faulks, Sebastian, 138
Faye, Alice, 141
Feldshuh, Tovah, 49
Ferrera, America, 158
Festinger, Robert, 61
Few Good Men, A, 64–66
Field, Sally, 157, 182
Field, Todd, 61
Fiennes, Joseph, 47
Fiennes, Ralph, 42
Fierstein, Harvey, 199
Fincher, David, 83
Finding Your Soul Mate Movies, 35–53
Finlay, Frank, 26
Finney, Albert, 140
First Wives Club, 46
Fisher, Antwone, 28, 29
Fisher, Frances, 102
Fisher King, The, 19, 57
Fitzgerald, Tara, 5, 183

Flanagan, Fionnula, 55
Fleming, Victor, 33
Flemyng, Jason, 166
Fletcher, Dexter, 137
Fletcher, Louise, 132, 133
Fonda, Henry, 144, 203, 204
Fonda, Jane, 139
Foote, Horton, 78
Ford, Glenn, 130, 131
Ford, Harrison, 172
Ford, John, 32, 203
Forever Friends, 44
Forrest Gump, 182–183
Fosse, Bob, 146
Foster, Jodie, 51, 83
Foul Play, 39
Fountainhead, The, 22, 69
Francis, Anne, 130
Franciscus, James, 114
Frank, Scott, 58
Fraser, Brendan, 39, 68, 89, 92, 190
Freeman, Morgan, 101, 103, 131
Frida, 17
Frontier House, 100
Frosty Returns, 74
Fry, Rosalie K., 107
Full Monty, The, 10–11
Furmaniak, Ralph, 119

Gambon, Michael, 138
Gandolfini, James, 70, 71
Gangs of New York, 12
Garber, Victor, 125
Gárdos, Éva, 96
Garland, Judy, 33, 82
Garner, James, 177, 178
Garofalo, Janeane, 44, 153, 154
Garr, Teri, 40
General's Daughter, The, 64
Gere, Richard, 39, 55, 146, 147, 202
Gersonides, 83
Gertz, Jami, 102, 103
Getting Back to Nature Movies, 98–119
Ghost World, 149
Giannini, Adriano, 105, 106
Gibson, Mel, 192
Gift, The, 2–3
Gilford, Jack, 179
Gilliam, Terry, 57
Gimme Shelter, 94–95
Glenn, Karen, 100
Glenn, Mark, 100
Glenn, Scott, 51
Godfather, The, 71
Godspell, 125
Goldman, William, 64, 122
Goldwyn, Tony, 96
Goodman, John, 74, 118
Goodwin, Raven, 156
Gordon, Ruth, 52, 53
Grace of My Heart, 2
Grant, Beth, 62, 63
Grant, Cary, 39
Grant, Hugh, 56, 183
Grant, Lee, 85

Grant, Susannah, 140
Grapes of Wrath, The, 203–204
Great Dictator, The, 27
Green, Seth, 127
Green, Tom, 41
Greene, David, 125
Greene, Graham, 92
Greenwood, Bruce, 105, 106
Greystoke: The Legend of Tarzan, Lord of the Apes, 112
Griffin, John Howard, 190, 191
Griffith, Kenneth, 183
Griffiths, Rachel, 18, 62, 63, 189
Grint, Rupert, 6
Groom, Winston, 182
Grualt, Jean, 123
Guest, Christopher, 11, 12, 63, 90, 173
Gulpilil, David, 30, 31
Guthrie, Arlo, 185, 186
Guttenberg, Steve, 179
Gyllenhaal, Jake, 156

G

Gable, Clark, 19, 23, 24
Gainsbourg, Charlotte, 3

H

Haid, Charles, 195
Haley, Jack, 33
Hall, Lee, 197
Hall, Michael C., 18
Hamm, Sam, 119
Hampton, Christopher, 92
Hancock, John Lee, 62
Hanks, Tom, 22, 38, 67, 68, 104, 161, 182, 183
Hannah, Daryl, 82

Happy Accidents, 49, 85

Harden, Marcia Gay, 136, 177

Harold and Maude, 52–53

Harrar, Heinrich, 117

Harris, Ed, 136, 195

Harris, Richard, 6, 11

Harris, Thomas, 51

Harris, Timothy, 128

Harrison, George, 88

Harrison, Rex, 49

Harry Potter and the Chamber of Secrets, 5, 11

Harry Potter and the Sorcerer's Stone, 6, 63

Hart, Ian, 183

Hart, Linda, 157, 158

Hartnett, Josh, 189

Harwood, Ronald, 26

Haskell, David, 125

Hawn, Goldie, 41, 45

Hayek, Salma, 17, 201

Haynes, Todd, 81

Haysbert, Dennis, 81

Hayward, Susan, 149

Haywood, Chris, 137

Heche, Anne, 195

Hedaya, Dan, 147

Hedren, Tippi, 41

Helgenberger, Marg, 140

Help!, 88

Henderson, Martin, 73

Hendra, Tony, 173, 174

Henry, Buck, 85, 147

Henry, O., 12

Hepburn, Audrey, 153

Hepburn, Katharine, 111

Herek, Stephen, 166

Herman, Mark, 4

Herndon, Venable, 185

Herr, Michael, 65

Herrera, Hayden, 17

Hershey, Barbara, 44, 126

Heston, Charlton, 49, 114, 121

Higgins, Colin, 52, 139

High School High, 129, 132–133

Hill, James, 110

Hilton, James, 115

Hirst, Michael, 47

Hoath, Florence, 193

Hockstetler, Joann, 8

Hoffman, Dustin, 122

Hoffman, Philip Seymour, 102

Holbrook, Hal, 122

Holland, Agnieszka, 195

Holm, Ian, 104, 112

Holmes, Katie, 2, 3

Holofcener, Nicole, 156

Hooks, Kevin, 25

Hopkins, Anthony, 51, 201

Hopper, Dennis, 65, 66

Horrocks, Jane, 4

Hours, The, 107, 148

How Green Was My Valley, 32–33, 201

Howard, John, 115, 116

Howard, Ron, 172, 179

Hudson, Hugh, 112

Hudson, Rock, 81

Hughes, John, 42

Hugo, Victor, 175

Huison, Steve, 10

Hulce, Tom, 104, 105

Human Comedy, The, 200

Humble Pie (Bev's Culinarytherapy), 151

Hunt, Helen, 102, 104

Hunt, Linda, 128, 129, 192

Hunter, Evan, 130

Hunter, Kim, 114

Hurt, William, 50, 67, 168, 169

Huston, Anjelica, 202

Huston, John, 23

Hutton, Timothy, 64

Huyck, Willard, 172

I Am Sam, 59–60

In Cold Blood, 79

In the Bedroom, 61

Inherit the Wind, 167–168

Interview, The, 51

Iris, 36

Itard, Jean, 123–124

It's a Wonderful Life, 82

Ittimangnaq, Zachary, 119

J

Jack, Wolfman, 172

Jackman, Hugh, 85

Jackson, Samuel L., 93, 94, 198

Jacobi, Derek, 137

Jaffe, Sam, 107, 115

Jagger, Mick, 94, 95

Jakoby, Don, 118

Jane Eyre, 3

Jesus Christ Superstar, 124–125

Jesus of Montreal, 126
Jeter, Michael, 2
Jeunet, Jean-Pierre, 43
Jewison, Norman, 124
Johansson, Scarlett, 96
Johnson, Celia, 131
Johnson, Kristine, 59
Johnson, Nunnally, 203
Johnson, Van, 200
Johnston, Becky, 117
Jones, Tommy Lee, 177, 178
Jonze, Spike, 75
Jorah, Samson, 119
Julia, Raul, 50

Kane, Carol, 48
Kapur, Shekhar, 47
Kassovitz, Mathieu, 43
Kate & Leopold, 85
Katz, Gloria, 172
Kaufman, Charlie, 75
Kaufman, Ken, 177
Kazan, Lainie, 36, 49
Kazantzakis, Nikos, 126
Kearney, Patrick, 60
Keen, Geoffrey, 110
Keen, Ken, 186
Keener, Catherine, 76, 142, 156, 157
Keep the River on Your Right, 99
Keeping It Real Movies, 145–159
Keitel, Harvey, 89, 126, 193, 194

Kelly, Gene, 167
Kennedy, Arthur, 3
Kidman, Nicole, 3, 13, 55, 107, 147, 148
Kindergarten Cop, 128
King, Stephen, 109
Kingsley, Dorothy, 149
Kinnear, Greg, 2, 38, 153, 154
Kinski, Nastassja, 96
Kirk, Laura, 152
Kiss of the Spider Woman, 50–51
Klausner, Howard, 177
Kletter, Richard, 119
Kloves, Steven, 6
Kluge, P.F., 97
Klugman, Jack, 144
Knowles, Beyoncé, 127
Koch, C.J., 192
Koepp, David, 83
Kovic, Ron, 162
Kozak, Harley Jane, 118
Kramer, Stanley, 167
Krause, Peter, 18
Kretschmann, Thomas, 26
Kromolowski, Jerzy, 110
Kruger, Ehren, 73
Kubrick, Stanley, 109
Kudrow, Lisa, 44, 45

L

L.A. Story, 19, 69
Ladies Room, The, 44
Lady, Steph, 104

LaGravanese, Richard, 57
Lahr, Bert, 33, 74
Lake, Diane, 17
Lally, Mick, 107
Lambert, Christopher, 112
Lane, Diane, 55
Lange, Jessica, 20
Langley, Noel, 33
Lasser, Louise, 153, 154
Lasseter, John, 161
Last Temptation of Christ, The, 126
László, Miklós, 38
Launer, Dale, 12
Laurant, Guillaume, 43
LaVoo, George, 158
Lawford, Myarn, 30, 31
Lawford, Ningali, 30, 31
Lawrence, Jerome, 167
Le Mat, Paul, 172
Lean on Me, 131
Leder, Mimi, 101
Lee, Ang, 163, 178
Lee, Haan, 178
Lee, Harper, 78, 79
Lee, Robert E., 167
LeGros, James, 76
Leigh, Mike, 137
Lemmon, Jack, 46
Leonard, Robert Sean, 48
Leoni, Téa, 101
Lerner, Carl, 190
Lerner, Gerda, 190
Leto, Jared, 83
Letting Go of Your Status Quo Movies, 160–180
Levine, Ted, 51
Levy, Eugene, 90

Lewis, Gary, 197
Lisa Picard is Famous, 152
Little Nicky, 89
Little Voice, 4–5
Little Women, 70
Living in Oblivion, 76, 77
Llewellyn, Richard, 32
Lloyd, Danny, 109
LoCash, Robert, 132
Lopez, Jennifer, 42
Lopez, Josefina, 158
Loren, Sophia, 13
Lost Horizon, 107, 115–116
Love Field, 81
Love Is All Around You
   Movies, 181–205
Lovely and Amazing, 156–157
Lovitz, Jon, 129, 132, 133
Lucas, George, 172
Lucas, Kevin, 137
Luescher, Christina, 119
Luke, Derek, 28
Luke, Keye, 168, 169
Lumet, Sidney, 97, 144
Lung, Sihung, 178
Lyne, Adrian, 55

m

MacDowell, Andie, 112
MacLaine, Shirley, 85, 86
Macy, William H., 24, 153, 154
Madigan, Amy, 136
Madonna, 105, 106
Magnificent Seven, The, 85

Mahal, Taj, 25
Maid in Manhattan, 42
Man Called Peter, A, 21
Mandel, Robert, 68
Mann, Alakina, 55
Manning, Taryn, 14
Manson, Marilyn, 121-122
Mantegna, Joe, 168, 169
March, Fredric, 167, 168
Margaret's Museum, 33, 56
Marshall, E.G., 144
Marshall, Frank, 118
Marshall, Garry, 44
Marshall, Rob, 146
Martin, Andrea, 36
Martin, Anne-Marie, 102
Martin, Steve, 19, 69
Martin, Tony, 51
Martinez, Olivier, 39, 55, 58
Marx, Groucho, 13
Mary Shelley's Frankenstein,
   104–105
Massey, Raymond, 69
Mathison, Melissa, 40
Matthau, Walter, 46, 84, 85
Maynard, Joyce, 147
Maysles, Albert, 94
Maysles, David, 94
McDowall, Roddy, 32, 114
McGann, Paul, 193
McGowan, Tom, 110
McGregor, Ewan, 4
McKean, Michael, 173, 174
McKenna, Virginia, 110
McLoughlin, Tom, 193
McNeice, Ian, 183
McQueen, Steve, 85
Meany, Colm, 183

Megna, John, 78
Mello, Tamara, 163
Menéndez, Ramón, 163
Merritt, Theresa, 149
Metcalf, Laurie, 161
Michell, Roger, 93
Midler, Bette, 12, 44, 46
Milius, John, 65
Miller, Arthur, 23
Miller, Emma, 8
Miller, Penelope Ann, 128
Minority Report, 58
Miracle Worker, The, 132
Mirkin, David, 44
Misérables, Les, 175–176
Misfits, The, 19, 23–24
Mitchell, Julian, 136
Mitchell, Kel, 153, 154
Modine, Matthew, 202, 203
Moisturizing Miracle for White
   Knuckles (Bev's
   Culinarytherapy), 80–81
Molina, Alfred, 17
Monaghan, Laura, 30, 31
Monahan, Craig, 51
Monger, Christopher, 183
Monger, Ivor, 183
Monroe, Marilyn, 23
Montalban, Ricardo, 114
Monty Python and the Holy Grail,
   21, 171
Monty Python's Life of Brian, 190
Moore, Demi, 64
Moore, Julianne, 81
Moore, Michael, 121–122
Moore, Thomas, 97
Morgan, Frank, 33, 200
Morissette, Alanis, 170

Morris, Jim, 62–63
Morris, John, 161
Morrow, Vic, 130
Mortimer, Emily, 156
Moulin Rouge, 148
Mount, Anson, 14
Mowat, Farley, 119
Mr. Destiny, 171
Mr. Holland's Opus, 132
Mr. Smith Goes to Washington, 201
Mueller-Stahl, Armin, 195
Mulligan, Robert, 78
Mulroney, Dermot, 76, 79, 80, 156
Musca, Tom, 163
My Big Fat Greek Wedding, 36–37, 49
My First Mister, 5, 48
Myers, Mike, 127, 176
Mystery Men, 11, 24, 39, 48, 85, 153–154

Naifeh, Steven, 136
Nathanson, Jeff, 67
Nava, Gregory, 17
Neame, Ronald, 133
Neeley, Ted, 124
Neeson, Liam, 175
Nelson, Jessie, 59
Never Been Kissed, 56
Never Cry Wolf, 119
Nicholls, Phoebe, 193

Nichols, Mike, 139
Nichols, Richard, 155
Nicholson, Jack, 64–66, 79, 109–110
Nijinsky, Vaslav, 137
Nine to Five, 139
No Way Out, 62
Norton, Edward, 17, 142, 143
Noth, Chris, 104
Now, Voyager, 69
Noyce, Phillip, 30, 92
Nyswaner, Ron, 22

Obradors, Jacqueline, 163
Odd Couple, The, 46–47, 84, 85
O'Donnell, Chris, 68
Oh, God, 171
O'Hara, Catherine, 84, 90, 91
O'Hara, Maureen, 32
Oleynik, Larisa, 96
Oliu, Ingrid, 158, 159
Olmos, Edward James, 131
Olsen, Christine, 30
Olyphant, Timothy, 166
Ontiveros, Lupe, 158
Orlean, Susan, 75
Osbourne, Ozzy, 89
Others, The, 3, 55–56
O'Toole, Peter, 193, 194
Owen, Reginald, 155

Pacino, Al, 71, 97
Pakula, Alan J., 122
Palin, Michael, 21
Panic Room, 83–84
Parkins, Barbara, 149, 150
Parton, Dolly, 139, 140
Paul, Elliot, 155
Paxton, Bill, 102
Paxton, Collin Wilcox, 78
Payne, Alexander, 79
Pearce, Richard, 20
Peck, Gregory, 78
Peña, Elizabeth, 163
Penn, Arthur, 185
Penn, Robin Wright, 182
Penn, Sean, 59, 110
Pérez, José, 171
Perrin, Nat, 141
Peters, Brock, 78
Petrie, Joan, 186
Pfeiffer, Michelle, 59, 81
Phifer, Mekhi, 132, 133
Philadelphia, 22–23
Phillips, Mackenzie, 172
Phoenix, Joachin, 147
Pianist, The, 26
Pidgeon, Walter, 32, 201
Pierson, Frank, 97
Pilkington, Doris, 30
Pitt, Brad, 117
Place in the Sun, A, 60–61
Planet of the Apes, 113–115
Pledge, The, 110
Plummer, Amanda, 57

Poitier, Sidney, 62, 81, 130, 132
Polanski, Roman, 26
Pollack, Sydney, 93
Pollock, 136–137
Ponicson, Darryl, 68
Portrait of a Lady, 148
Posey, Parker, 38, 90, 91
Power of One Movies, 120–144
Prime of Miss Jean Brodie, The, 10, 131, 133–135
Producers, The, 27
Proft, Pat, 132
Puig, Manuel, 50
Pullman, Bill, 12
Pushing Hands, 178–179

Quaid, Dennis, 62, 81
Quiet American, The, 92–93
Quigley Down Under, 165
Quinn, Aidan, 104
Quinn, Patricia, 185

Rabbit-Proof Fence, 30–31
Radcliffe, Daniel, 5, 6
Radner, Gilda, 111
Raimi, Sam, 2
Ranft, Joe, 161

Real Women Have Curves, 158–159
Redding, Stan, 67
Redford, Robert, 122
Redgrave, Vanessa, 101
Reed, Carol, 49
Reed, Donna, 200
Reed, Pamela, 128
Reeves, Keanu, 2, 21
Reiner, Rob, 64, 84, 173, 175
Reinhold, Judge, 12
Reitman, Ivan, 128
Rennison, Colleen, 157
Reno, Kelly, 40
Resnick, Adam, 142
Resnick, Patricia, 139
Reubens, Paul, 153, 154
Rhimes, Shonda, 14
Rhys, Paul, 136
Ribisi, Giovanni, 2
Rice, Tim, 124
Rich, Mike, 62
Richards, Keith, 94
Richardson, Natasha, 189
Richardson, Ralph, 112
Rickles, Don, 161
Rickman, Alan, 6, 63, 84, 170, 189
Ring, The, 73
Ripoll, María, 163
Riskin, Robert, 115
Rispoli, Michael, 195
Ritchie, Guy, 105
Ritt, Martin, 25
Ritter, Thelma, 23
Roach, Jay, 127
Robards, Jason, 22, 122
Roberts, Julia, 140

Robin Hood: Prince of Thieves, 84
Robson, Mark, 149
Rock Star, 166
Rodriguez, Paul, 163
Romano, John, 195
Romy and Michelle's High School Reunion, 44–45
Rookie, The, 62–63
Rooney, Mickey, 40, 200
Rose, Reginald, 144
Rosenberg, Jeanne, 40
Roth, Eric, 182
Roth, Tim, 136
Rowling, J.K., 6
Rubin, Bruce Joel, 101
Rudolph the Red Nosed Reindeer, 153
Ruehl, Mercedes, 57
RuPaul, 6
Rush, Geoffrey, 45, 47, 153, 154, 175, 176
Russell, Kurt, 41, 139
Ruthless People, 12–13
Ryan, Meg, 38
Ryder, Winona, 70, 198, 199
Ryerson, Florence, 33

Saks, Gene, 46
Saldana, Zoe, 14
Salem, Murray, 128
Sampi, Everlyn, 30
Sansbury, Tianna, 30, 31

Saperstein, David, 179
Sarandon, Susan, 45
Sargent, Alvin, 55
Saroyan, William, 200
Savoca, John, 144
Sayles, John, 107
Schamus, James, 163, 178
Schank, Mike, 186
Scheider, Roy, 21
Schenkkan, Robert, 92
Schiff, Richard, 59
Schiff, Robin, 44
Schimmels, Tom, 186
Schneebaum, Tobias, 99
School Ties, 68–69
Schrader, Leonard, 50
Schrader, Paul, 126
Schwarzenegger, Arnold, 90, 128, 129
Scorsese, Martin, 126
Scott, George C., 103
Scotti, Tony, 149, 150
Secret of Roan Inish, The, 107–108
Sedgwick, Kyra, 162
Seigner, Françoise, 123
Seiter, William A., 141
Selleck, Tom, 165
Sellers, Peter, 27
Seltzer, David, 196
Seven Years in Tibet, 117
Shadowlands, 201
Shadyac, Tom, 196
Shapiro, David, 99
Shapiro, Laurie, 99
Shearer, Harry, 173–175
Sheekman, Arthur, 141
Sheen, Martin, 65

Shelley, Mary, 104
Shepard, Sam, 20
Sheridan, Richard, 107, 108
Shilts, Randy, 202
Shining, The, 109
Shining Out Movies, 1–15
Shop Around the Corner, The, 38
Shulman, Arnold, 202
Sid Vicious, 41
Sigal, Clancy, 17
Silence of the Lambs, The, 51
Silkwood, 139
Silvan, Delia, 137
Simon, Neil, 46
Simon Birch, 194
Sinise, Gary, 182
Six Feet Under, 18–19
Slater, Helen, 12
Smith, Charles Martin, 119, 172
Smith, Chris, 186
Smith, Gregory White, 136
Smith, Harold Jacob, 167
Smith, Ian Michael, 194
Smith, Maggie, 6, 10, 131, 133-135
Smith, Sukie, 137
Snape, William, 10, 11
Snyder, Deb, 178
Sobieski, Leelee, 5
Soderbergh, Steven, 140
Sokolow, Alec, 161
Somers, Suzanne, 172
Sopranos, The, 70–71
Sorkin, Aaron, 64
Sorvino, Mira, 44, 45
Sounder, 25
Space Cowboys, 177–178

Spacek, Sissy, 61
Spark, Muriel, 133
Spears, Britney, 14–15
Spibey, Dina, 18
Spielberg, Steven, 58, 62, 67
Splash, 82
Spottiswoode, Roger, 202
Stahl, Nick, 61
Stand and Deliver, 131
Stanley, Kim, 79
Stanton, Andrew, 161
Stapleton, Maureen, 179
Star Trek V, 171
Steambath, 171
Steel Magnolias, 140
Steenburgen, Mary, 22
Steinbeck, John, 203
Sterling, Mindy, 127
Stevens, George, 60
Stewart, Donald Ogden, 155
Stewart, James, 38, 62, 82
Stewart, Jon, 142
Stewart, Kristen, 83
Stiller, Ben, 39, 85, 153, 154
Stockwell, John, 166
Stone, Irving, 49
Stone, Oliver, 162
Stowaway, 141–142
Stowe, Madeleine, 64
Strathairn, David, 194
Streep, Meryl, 75, 85, 86, 139
Strick, Wesley, 118
Studi, Wes, 48
Sturridge, Charles, 193
Sukowa, Barbara, 195
Sullavan, Margaret, 38
Sunset Boulevard, 91

Susann, Jacqueline, 149
Sutherland, Donald, 177, 178
Sutherland, Kiefer, 64
Suzuki, Kôji, 73
Swank, Hilary, 2
Swanson, Gloria, 91
Swept Away, 105–106
Szpilman, Wladyslaw, 26, 27

Takahashi, Hiroshi, 73
Talk of the Town, The, 12
Tally, Ted, 51
Tandy, Jessica, 179
Tape, 48
Tate, Sharon, 149, 150
Tatou, Audrey, 43
Taylor, Chap, 93
Taylor, Elizabeth, 41, 60
Taylor, Jim, 79
Taylor, Mick, 94
Taymor, Julie, 17
Tebelak, John-Michael, 125
Temple, Shirley, 141
Ten Commandments, The, 170
The Sun Will Come Out Tomorrow Pancakes (Bev's Culinarytherapy), 29–30
Third Miracle, The, 195
This Is Spinal Tap, 63, 84, 173–175
Thomas, Anna, 17

Thomas Crown Affair, The, 19
Thompson, Caroline, 198
Thompson, Mike, 196
Thompson, Susanna, 196
Thornton, Billy Bob, 2
Thorpe, Richard, 33
Thurman, Uma, 175, 176
Titanic, 91, 102, 103
To Die For, 147, 148
To Kill a Mockingbird, 78
To Sir, with Love, 132
Todd, Richard, 21
Tolkin, Michael, 93, 101
Tomei, Marisa, 61, 85
Tomlin, Lily, 139, 202
Topsy-Turvy, 137
Torn, Rip, 85, 86
Tortilla Soup, 163
Tortilla Soup (Bev's Culinarytherapy), 164–165
Towne, Robert, 112
Toy Story, 161
Tracy, Spencer, 74, 167, 168
Travers, Bill, 110
Travolta, John, 64
Traylor, William, 74
Troyer, Verne, 127
Truffaut, François, 123
Turner, Barbara, 136
Turner, Kathleen, 157
Turturro, John, 2
12 Angry Men, 144
Twister, 102, 103
Tyson, Cecily, 25

Unfaithful, 39, 55, 58
Usher, Kinka, 153

Valley of the Dolls, 149–150
Van Sant, Gus, 147
Vardalos, Nia, 36, 37
Veidt, Conrad, 155, 156
Verbinski, Gore, 73
Verdon, Gwen, 179
Vetere, Richard, 195
Vincent and Theo, 136
Von Detten, Erik, 161
Von Sydow, Max, 58
Von Zernack, Danielle, 76

Wade, Kevin, 42
Wagner, Robert, 127
Wahlberg, Mark, 115, 166
Waiting for Guffman, 11, 12, 90–91
Walken, Christopher, 67
Walker, Lucy, 8
Wallach, Eli, 23
Walters, Jack, 184

Walters, Julie, 197
Wang, Bo Z., 178, 179
Wang, Hui-Ling, 163
Wang, Lai, 178
Wang, Wayne, 42
Wangchuk, Jamyang Jamtsho, 117
Warden, Jack, 144
Washington, Denzel, 22, 28, 29
Washington Square, 135
Watkins, Maurine Dallas, 146
Watson, Emma, 6
Watts, Charlie, 94
Watts, Naomi, 73
Weaver, Sigourney, 192
Weaving, Hugo, 51
Weingrod, Herschel, 128
Weir, Peter, 192
Welch, Raquel, 163
Welch, Tahnee, 179
Welsh, Kenneth, 56
Wertmüller, Lina, 105, 106
West, Simon, 64
Whalen, Sean, 56
What's New Pussycat?, 27
Whedon, Joss, 161
When-the-Chips-Are-Down
   Chocolate Chip Cookies
   (Bev's Culinarytherapy), 188
Whitaker, Forest, 83

Whitmore, James, 190
Widmark, Richard, 62
Wiest, Dianne, 59, 198, 199
Wild Child, The, 123–124
Wilkening, Catherine, 126
Wilkinson, Tom, 10, 61
Willard, Fred, 90
Williams, Al, 118
Williams, Cindy, 172
Williams, Robin, 19, 57, 142
Williamson, Mykelti, 182
Willis, Bruce, 41
Wilson, Michael, 60
Winfield, Paul, 25
Winslet, Kate, 36, 102
Winters, Shelley, 60
Wittliff, William D., 20, 40
Wizard of Oz, The, 33–34, 74, 82
Wolf, Dick, 68
Woman's Face, A, 155–156
Wong, B.D., 117
Wood, Charles, 36
Wood, Elijah, 101
Woodward, Bob, 122–123
Woolf, Edgar Allan, 33
Wyatt, Jane, 115
Wyman, Bill, 94
Wyman, Jane, 81

Year of Living Dangerously, The, 192
Yen, Do Thi Hai, 92
Yglesias, Rafael, 175
Yoakam, Dwight, 83
Yoder, Faron, 8
York, Dick, 167
York, Michael, 127
Young, Nedrick, 167
Young, Robert, 141
You've Got Mail, 38
Yutzy, Gerald, 8

Z

Zebrowski, Michal, 26
Zellweger, Renée, 146, 198
Zemeckis, Robert, 62, 104, 182
Zeta-Jones, Catherine, 146
Zucker, David, 12, 132
Zwerin, Charlotte, 94
Zwick, Joel, 36